# WiNE GENiUS

# WïNE GENïUS

## JANICE FUHRMAN

MQP

Published by **MQ Publications Limited**

12 The Ivories, 6–8 Northampton Street

London N1 2HY

TEL: 020 7359 2244

FAX: 020 7359 1616

EMAIL: mail@mqpublications.com

WEBSITE: www.mqpublications.com

SERIES EDITOR: **abi rowsell**

EDITOR: **yvonne deutch**

DESIGN: **balley design associates**

ILLUSTRATION: **tom morris, karen hood**

GENIUS CARICATURE: **chris garbutt**

ISBN: 1 84072 540 0

1 3 5 7 9 0 8 6 4 2

Printed in China

# contents

# Introduction

Although the following pages of *Wine Genius* are filled with my thoughts, experiences, ideas, and tips about wine, you might detect an underlying subversive note. That's because, quite simply, my aim is to demystify wine lore. Do you believe you have to be educated about every aspect of chocolate or cheese to enjoy them? Of course not. Then why should this be necessary with wine? It's still widely assumed by many in the wine world that you need special expertise to enjoy wine, but in fact it's just one of many beverages we drink. Wine can be simple or it can be complex, well-crafted or mediocre, but at its core the experience of tasting and enjoying wine is subjective—everyone will experience it in a different and unique way.

In *Wine Genius* no one is dictating which wines you should drink, or how, when, or why, you should enjoy wine. On the contrary, what you'll find here is a direct, useful, easy-to-understand guide to all the information and vocabulary you will encounter at the wine store, in wine magazines, on wine labels and at restaurants. This way, anyone, including you, can become a genuine wine genius, simply by being guided toward your own discoveries.

Here you'll find short informative, pointers covering everything you need to know about wine—plus lots of extra tips and bits of interesting "wine buff" information. And *Wine Genius* is user-friendly, too—you can dip straight into any section that interests you, and go directly to what you want to know.

So, now you're all set to become a wine genius—why not pull up a chair, pop a cork, pour yourself a delicious glass, and read these encouraging tips to get you started?

- Relax about wine! It's about pleasure, not a contest to see who knows most!

- Try many types of wine and you will find something that suits your taste. If you know you don't like champagne, for instance, don't give up. Just try red wine or white, rosé, port, or sherry. There are so many types of wine made in so many styles today that you will probably find something you'll want to have around for life.

- Banish all wine fear! If it catches your fancy, dare to ask for a wine that you don't know how to pronounce. It's the only way you will learn and taste something new. Be brave!

- Rely on help. Wine merchants, restaurant servers, *sommeliers*, even grocery store clerks, all know something about the products they sell and serve, so ask them for help about what to drink, what to match with your food or your mood, what to give as a gift, and what to collect. Don't be shy!

- Loosen up about the rules and let taste be your guide! Yes, there are lots of them—but the most important is that you choose what tastes good to you.

- Benefit from the fact that there are so many wine regions around the world. They are turning out such quantities of good-to-excellent wines that competition among wine producers is at an all-time high. You don't have to spend a lot of money to enjoy good wine.

- Learn the few rules necessary to know to store your wine properly— whether you have two bottles or 200. It doesn't take a lot of fancy and expensive equipment and proper storage will protect the bottles you have and ensure your enjoyment of them.

- Entertain with wine. It is perfect for putting people at ease with each other and will jump-start any party. What's more it's highly versatile and can be reasonably priced. You can mix it with fruit, sparkling water or juices, or choose a special wine to complement the food on your party menu.

- Enhance your wine with food and your food with wine. Wine is a perfectly natural companion for food, and increases its pleasure.

- Drink locally. You don't have to travel to enjoy wines from around the world because they are being exported everywhere. But when you *do* travel, try the local wines and brews. They have evolved with the local cuisine and are usually uniquely suited to it. So don't drink California wine when you're in Greece, or vice versa.

See? It's not that difficult. All you need is an open mind, and a willingness to try all kinds of wines—that's what makes a real wine genius.

# chapter 1

# getting acquainted with wine

There's something about the subject of wine that seems to scare people. But that's completely unnecessary—you really don't have to be nervous. If someone tells you that there is such a thing as a "perfect" wine, that's just their personal opinion. Certainly, there are fine wines, sweet wines, dry wines, and sparkling wines, but how good a particular bottle is remains a matter of subjective taste. You either like the flavor of the wine on your palate, or you don't. Essentially, the first step in feeling comfortable with wine is defining what you like and finding the particular wines that suit your tastes. As you explore, you'll ask yourself lots of questions. Is there something wrong about preferring fruity wines to dry? Is red wine better than white? What is a fortified wine? Does it matter if you drink sweet wine with a main course? All this anxiety will diminish when you begin to regard wine more as a familiar beverage rather than as a degree subject in gourmet expertise. For instance, you probably know whether you object to drinking flat soda or warm beer. And presumably, you've no problem discussing the rival merits of lemonade and Coke? Viewed from that standpoint, wine is simply a beverage to be enjoyed —and what you prefer to drink is entirely up to you.

## What is wine?

Wine is one of the greatest sources of pleasure that human beings have devised. It's not just a beverage but something mysterious, complex, intellectual, and wonderful that springs from something quite ordinary—the grape. Agriculture, science, and art are all called upon in the making of the magical potion we call wine, which has been with us for 5,000 years, inspiring the muses, fueling fellowship, and adding to our enjoyment of life. Special wine grapes, a new vintage each year, are grown, harvested, pressed into wine, aged, and bottled. So, at one level, while wine is simply fermented grape juice, at another, it has become a great art form over thousands of years, a nectar that nourishes the dreams, festive occasions, and important milestones of life.

## Get out there and explore

Always be positive in your approach to tasting new wines, and be willing to explore the wide selection of types that are available. You'll invariably find something that suits your taste, and the road to discovery will bring you great pleasure in itself. The more open-minded you are about wine, the more confident you'll become. It's tempting to get stuck in a rut, and cling to the security of choosing the same familiar wine because it feels "safe." Fine, but then you're missing out on all the wonderful and varied delights that are out there waiting to be enjoyed. And if a particular wine is not to your taste, so what? Don't let that put you off. Move on, and try something else. There are so many types of wine to discover—all those wonderful reds, rosés, and whites, still and sparkling wines, ports and sherries—so you'll have lots of fun experimenting.

## A great choice of wine styles

Explore the many different styles of wine on offer. The reason wine is never boring is because winemakers make it in so many styles, using different grapes and different methods to make still and sparkling wines in red, white, and rosé. One winemaker might create a style of wine that is lush, full-bodied, and unctuous, while another produces wine that is crisp, clean, and light. Wine can have a low or high alcohol content, and a low or high price tag. It can show off the flavors of the grape or get its character from other added flavors, such as oak from the barrels it is aged in, or from herbs or other fruit additives. Today, wine is so available and affordable that anyone can drink it—and no one needs superior knowledge to enjoy it. So, cheers!

I'm always asking people what wine they like best. So, like me, reap the benefit from other people's experience and enthusiasm, and learn the art of asking for advice. For instance, check out whether that on-the-ball friend of yours has come across a good wine lately, and is happy to recommend it. And, when you're browsing along the shelves of your local wine merchant and you're attracted to a wine, take it up to the counter and ask for an informal opinion. You may have hit upon exactly the perfect choice there and then, or it might be a good start in the right direction. Restaurant servers, *sommeliers* (wine waiters), even grocery-store clerks all know something about the products they sell and serve, so it is natural to ask them for help about what to drink, what to match with your food or your mood, what to give as a gift, and what to collect. Don't be shy!

## Start with the grape

Acquire some basic knowledge about wine; apart from being useful in itself, it will give you more confidence. For instance, many people think that wine grapes are the same as the ones we eat. Not true. In fact, around 99.9 percent of wine grapes belong to a sub-genus called Vitis vinifera. Most wine grapes originated in Europe and central Asia and have been imported to other wine regions of the world. They are usually smaller than table grapes and they always contain seeds. Although wine grapes are grown around the world on almost every continent, different types benefit from certain types of soils and climates.

## Can you learn to make wine yourself?

The answer is, yes, you can. If you're a wannabe winemaker, you'll be pleased to discover that hobbyists, sometimes called "home winemakers" do exist. They make wine at home, educating themselves about winemaking from books or friends and investing in equipment that fits into their basements or garages. In fact, a few of the most sought-after wines in America and Europe grew out of simple garage or warehouse settings, and are now known as "boutique wines." Wineries usually hire winemakers who have been trained at universities in enology or fermentation science. But many good winemakers are basically self-taught and learn on the job, starting out by tending the vines or tending to equipment in the winery.

Never underestimate your own sense of taste and discrimination—if a wine seems really good to you, then go ahead and enjoy it. That's the point of drinking wine—it should bring you great pleasure and enjoyment. That's not to say that it's also a good idea to explore widely, experiment with different types of wine, and keep an open mind. So, listen to others, but trust your own taste also. Even pros don't always "know" what's best. Wine tasting is highly subjective. Your opinion of a wine is the one that counts—not a wine writer's, a wine collector's, or the vendor's. The experts seldom agree, anyway. If you asked ten winemakers, wine writers, or other wine professionals their opinions of a dozen wines, each would produce a different opinion about the tastes they perceive, the wine's structure, and even its color!

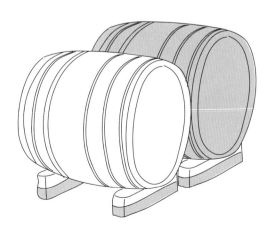

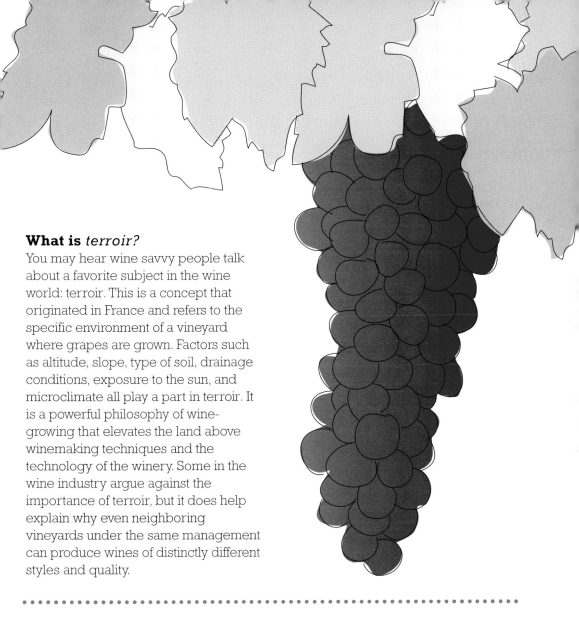

## What is *terroir?*

You may hear wine savvy people talk about a favorite subject in the wine world: terroir. This is a concept that originated in France and refers to the specific environment of a vineyard where grapes are grown. Factors such as altitude, slope, type of soil, drainage conditions, exposure to the sun, and microclimate all play a part in terroir. It is a powerful philosophy of wine-growing that elevates the land above winemaking techniques and the technology of the winery. Some in the wine industry argue against the importance of terroir, but it does help explain why even neighboring vineyards under the same management can produce wines of distinctly different styles and quality.

## Red wine

Choose a red wine if you prefer a richer, weightier wine with deeper flavors than white. Reds are made from special red or "black" grapes, such as Cabernet Sauvignon, Merlot, Pinot Noir, or Zinfandel. The deep colors and flavors of most red wines result from the grape skins and seeds soaking together with the grape juice for days or weeks, and from aging in oak barrels. Tannins, found to a much greater degree in red wines than whites, give red wine its astringent quality and allow for them to age long into the future. Although most red wines can be enjoyed right away, some—usually the more expensive ones—will improve with age. If properly stored, most Pinot Noir and Zinfandel will improve in five to ten years and Cabernet Sauvignon will continue to improve ten to fifteen years after the date on the bottle.

getting acquainted with wine

## When it's hot, it's not...good

Have you been told to drink red wines at room temperature? That's the conventional wisdom, but in hot weather or modern overheated homes in winter, that rule doesn't always make sense. A good idea is to refrigerate a red wine for about twenty minutes before serving it. It will lower the wine's temperature to about 65°F/18°C)—what used to be "room temperature" in many European countries in the days before central heating. The bottle should be cool to the touch. When reds (or whites) are too cold, their aromas and flavors are masked. When red wines are too warm, you tend to taste alcohol more than anything else. If red wine is too cold, allow it to sit at room temperature for about thirty minutes. To avoid warming the wine while drinking it, hold your wine glass by its stem, not the bowl. (See Chapter 7 for more details on wine temperatures.)

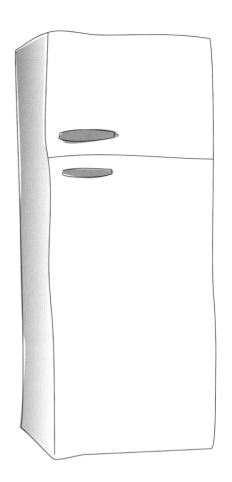

## White wine

It's called white wine because it's made from white (well, okay: green) grapes. Chardonnay, Sauvignon Blanc, Pinot Grigio, and Riesling are among the world's most popular white grape varieties. After the grapes are pressed to collect their juices, they are not fermented in contact with their skins the way red wines are. One exception to this is blanc de noirs, a white or lightly tinted Champagne made from the juice of black grapes. If there is a tint to the wine, it comes from pigments in the grape skins, but the skins are removed before the wine turns a deeper color. White wines are usually lighter, fresher, and more delicate than reds and are a good place to start if you are new to drinking wine. White wines can be aged in oak barrels—for a richer, fuller-bodied wine, as is often done with "New World" Chardonnay (e.g. from California and Australia)—or in large stainless steel tanks, which renders a crisp, clean profile to the wine.

## Chill out

Nothing hits the spot like a refreshing glass of chilled white wine. Be sure to serve all white wines cold, but not so cold that their aromas and flavors are killed. Refrigerate white wines for up to two hours before serving. Don't have two hours to ice your wine to its optimum temperature? Then give it an ice bath: sit the wine in a bath of ice and water for about thirty minutes. When you remove bottles from the refrigerator or ice bucket, let them sit awhile before opening and serving—a few minutes in the warm months and up to fifteen minutes in the winter. Most white wines do not age well and are intended for drinking within two to three years after the vintage date. (See Chapter 7 for more details on wine temperatures for serving.)

Which is better, white or red? Don't be confused by wine know-it-alls who claim that red wines are more sophisticated than whites. Many wine connoisseurs say reds are more "serious" than whites; they drink mostly reds and concentrate on collecting them, which pushes their prices up. But saying that red wines are a better choice than whites is like comparing a beach vacation to a ski trip. One is not "better" than the other; they're simply different. Because of their tannins, reds age longer and better than whites, giving wine collectors the chance to see them evolve with age. But true wine-lovers also enjoy many types of wines. Just as a food-lover wouldn't dream of eating steak every night for dinner, a lover of wine is someone who tries and likes many kinds of wines. So, enjoy exploring them.

## Leave me alone—I'm sensitive

Who has the more sensitive taste buds? Do people who prefer strong red wines possess the best? No. People who enjoy softer, fruitier wines, such as white Zinfandel, might have the most sensitive palates of all. A wine like this goes down easily, has no bitterness and none of that mouth-puckering sensation that comes with many so-called "serious" red wines. So, people with sensitive palates choose wines that are not as abusive to their taste buds as strong red wines would be. Taste in wine is like eyesight; people rarely have twenty-twenty vision. Some are color-blind, nearsighted or farsighted. Our tongues have blind spots, too. Some are more sensitive than others, some lack the ability to taste bitterness, while in others, even a tiny level of bitterness will taste unpleasant.

Why should you be stereotyped? Although many restaurants report that women tend to order white wines and men tend to order reds more often, a major California winery says its surveys have found that people can't be pigeonholed when it comes to wine preferences. Sweet wines such as white Zinfandel have a reputation for being "girlie wines," "ladies' wines," or "college kids' wines," but the winery has found that sweet-wine consumption is very evenly spread between men and women. So next time someone thinks they can predict what you'll drink, quote the survey findings back at them, and order what you like with confidence!

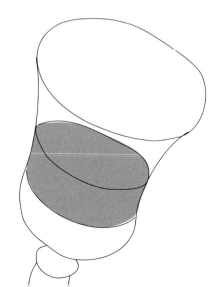

## In the pink

Most rosé wines are made from red or black grapes in much the same way red wines are, except their skins are allowed to soak with the grape juice for only a short time—just enough to tint the juice a pink or light red color. Dry rosé wines are often made from Pinot Noir, Cabernet Franc, and other red grape varieties. And sweeter versions, usually called "blush wines" in the U.S. are often made from the Zinfandel or Merlot grape and sold as "White Zinfandel" or "White Merlot." Rosés or blush wines are not for aging, but for drinking young. Unlike red wines, serve rosé wines well-chilled. They are most popular in the summer, but if you like them there is no reason not to drink them all year round. Rosé is also known as rosado in Spain and rosato in Italy.

> ### wine buff
>
> Despite all this talk of grapes, the main ingredient in wine is water. The average bottle of wine also contains sugar, carbon dioxide, chemical compounds that produce aromas, alcohol, acids, vitamins, and proteins, among other properties.

## "Green" wines

Can you do your bit to protect the environment and enjoy nice wines? Yes. Seek out organic wines or ones made from sustainably farmed (translation: kind to the environment) grapes. Organic wines are made with organic farming methods in the vineyards and minimum chemical intervention during the winemaking process (some sulphur dioxide, a preservative, is allowed by some organic regulators). Natural farming and increasing sensitivity to the environment are gaining in popularity with wine grape-growers around the world, and organic wines are made in Australia, Argentina, Canada, Chile, France, Italy, South Africa, Spain, New Zealand, and the United States, among others. Wine grape-growers use good bugs to go after bad bugs in the vineyards, organic materials to fight mildew, and natural materials instead of herbicides and pesticides. Their goal is to improve both their wines and the environment. There is no international standard, however, so different countries—and in the U.S., different states—have different definitions of just what constitutes an organic wine.

## Pop! Oops—got you!

There's nothing better than soaking in a hot bath full of bubbles—except when it's accompanied by a glass of bubbles. Ah, Champagne. The tiny bubbles in Champagne or sparkling wine are produced from putting the wine through two fermentations, the second one in the bottle. Often reserved for celebrations such as weddings, anniversaries, and New Year's Eve, Champagne is a festive drink, but it also goes with any meal at any time of the year. Its name comes from the specific region of France where the classic method of making Champagne, known as the méthode champenoise, originated (see Chapter 6). Although there are several other, less expensive, ways of putting bubbles in wine, méthode champenoise is widely considered the highest-quality wine.

## A wine by any other name...

Have you ever been confused by the range of names you have heard used for "Champagne"? There's sparkling wine in the U.S., cava in Spain, Sekt in Germany, and Prosecco and Asti in Italy. Then, of course, there's French Champagne. Most high-end American producers of Champagnes call their products "sparkling wine" to differentiate them from the wines made in the Champagne region of France, but they are usually made using the same French method. In Spain, the word cava refers to the vast underground cellars in which bottles of Spanish sparkling wine are usually aged. The majority of it, too, is made using the méthode champenoise, although with very different grape varieties. Cava usually costs less than French Champagne and is a great substitute when it's your boyfriend's birthday but you can't afford the real thing. Champagne is best when served cold. While you are enjoying your first glasses, keep the bottle chilled in an ice bucket or return it to the refrigerator until you need a refill.

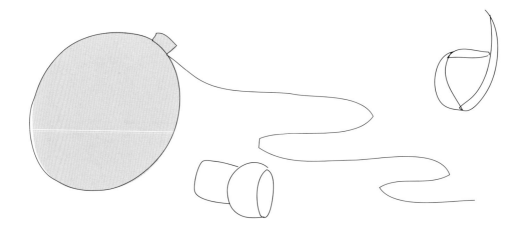

## A pair of whats?

When you're having friends over for dinner, why not welcome them with a glass of wine that is specially designed to enjoy before eating? Aperitifs are meant for drinking in relatively small amounts before a meal to whet the appetite for what is to come. A glass of light white wine, Champagne, a kir or kir royale, or perhaps fortified wines such as sherry, Dubonnet, (laced with herbs and quinine), or vermouth, a fortified wine flavored with spices, herbs and fruits, are popularly served around the world as aperitifs.

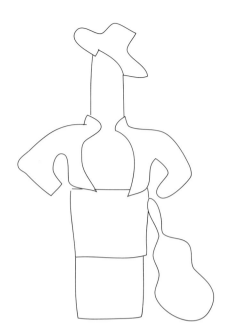

## Ma sherry...

If you always serve up the same aperitifs, why not go a little more trendy and take a tip from the experts? Look for a sherry from Spain, where it originated in the Jerez de la Frontera area. Sherry is the aperitif in Spain, and it is a popular aperitif around the world, too. Sherry is made from adding neutral grape spirits to a base wine once its fermentation stops, then blending meticulously for several years in a complicated cask system known as a solera. There are different styles of sherry, so try them all to see which you prefer: Fino and Manzanilla are delicate, dry, and crisp; Amontillado has a nuttier taste; Oloroso is rich and full flavored, and is made in sweet and dry styles. There is also the incredibly rich sherry known simply as "PX" (for Pedro Ximénez, the grape it comes from), which is often so rich that the Spanish pour it over ice cream!

## An island treat

Now that you are getting somewhat more adventurous with your choice of aperitifs, here's another one to tempt you. Madeira is a fortified wine made in a number of styles ranging from Malmsey, which is sweet and rich in flavor, to Sercial, which is dry and tangy. All Madeiras have a distinctive flavor and aroma and, like ports, have a long shelf life. Madeira comes from an island that is a Portuguese possession. It has been made since the eighteenth century, and is unusual in that is often placed in warm rooms (or attic rafters), where temperatures can reach up to 105°F/ 40°C, to age in order to achieve its special "cooked" flavor. Serve it as an aperitif or, if you're a keen chef, try using it in your cooking, especially if you want to give a deep, luscious flavor to your sauces and gravies.

Have you tried port lately? If you automatically think it's a drink for the older generation, think again. When you're in the mood for a sweet, rich, strong wine after dinner that will go well with a cigar or with chocolates, port is just perfect. It's a so-called "fortified wine," which means grape spirits are added to a base wine during its fermentation. It originated in Portugal, where it received its name, but port-style wines are now made around the world. Ruby and tawny ports are aged in wood barrels, and vintage port is sometimes aged in the bottle for ten to forty years, and vary from robustly fruity to subtle, dry, and nutty.

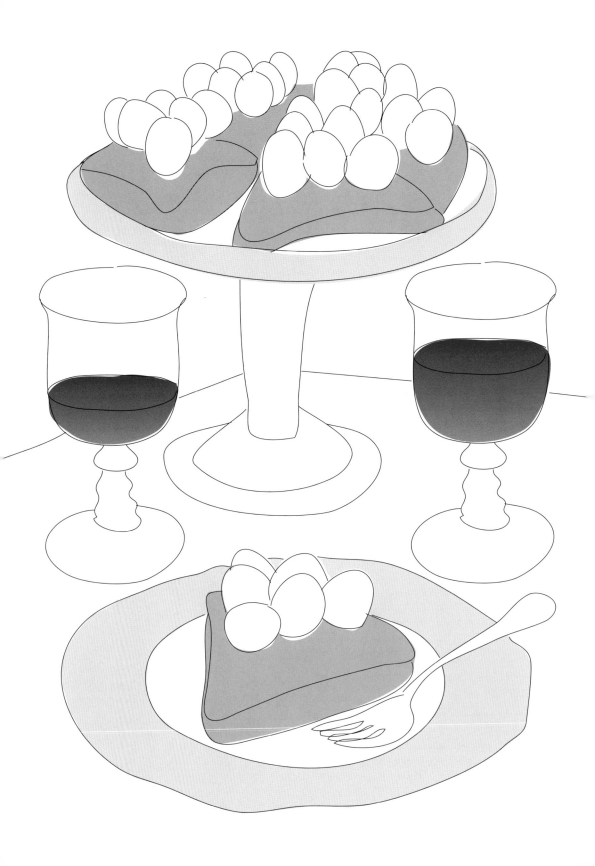

## A sweet finish

Sweet and chic? But of course! A beautifully made dessert wine is a masterpiece of the winemaker's art. And by choosing a really good dessert wine, you'll be showing your own good taste. Next time you're in a wine store, spend some time looking at the dessert wines on offer. Some are the result of a special process called "noble rot" or botrytis: a fungus that infects grapes and concentrates their sweetness. They are often called "late–harvest wines" in the United States, while in other countries, particularly Germany and France, "late-harvest" wines are made with or without botrytized grapes. Dessert wines are usually made from Riesling, Sauvignon Blanc, Sémillon, and Gewürztraminer grape varieties. They taste rich and honeyed and possess dense textures. Other sweet wines drunk at the end of a meal, such as those made from the Moscato grape, are picked at a normal ripeness with normal sugar levels, but fermentation is stopped before all the sugar has been converted to alcohol, resulting in a sweeter wine. Sometimes, this kind of wine can also have a bit of a fizz on the tongue.

## Extreme wines

If you want a show-stopping dessert wine, choose an ice wine (Eiswein in Germany, where it originated). It is deep and rich in color, aroma, and flavor. Riesling grapes are commonly used to make ice wines, which are served cold—but hold the ice! Originally from Germany and Austria, ice wine is also made in Canada and a few other cold regions. Grapes for this dessert wine are picked in the dead of winter while the grapes are frozen on the vines. When they are pressed, most of the water content of the berries is left behind in the form of ice crystals and the remaining juice is highly concentrated and intensely aromatic. Because of the extra care taken to produce ice wines and the fact that making it is a risky proposition, they tend to be high-priced.

## A blessing in every bottle

Traditional Kosher wines used in Jewish religious ceremonies can be excessively syrupy, but many kosher wines today come from the great wine regions of the world such as Bordeaux, California, South Africa, and Australia. The wines are made using the same kind of high-quality grapes from these regions and most of the same winemaking techniques employed with non-kosher wines. The difference is that kosher wines (kosher is a Hebrew word for "proper") are made according to an ancient set of rules from Judaism which, among other things, excludes non-Jews and women from the winemaking process and, in many cases, calls for briefly heating the wines.

### The debate continues

Numerous medical studies suggest that wine may be helpful to your health if drunk in moderation. The most famous, the so-called "French Paradox" study, cited lower rates of heart disease in France than in the U.S.—even though the French eat a diet that is high in fat. Researchers said this was due to the much greater amount of wine, especially red wine, drunk by the French. Various scientific studies have supported the idea that moderate alcohol consumption can be effective in preventing some of the world's most persistent maladies, including high blood pressure, heart disease, cancer, breast cancer, poor cognition, the common cold, stress, and obesity. And ethanol, an element of wine, is said to raise levels of HDL (the so-called "good cholesterol") in our bodies. But remember that the experts always use the phrase "in moderation".

### Better red than white?

The answer is "not necessarily." The French Paradox study suggests that red wines are more heart-healthy than white wines. That's because red wines have more polyphenols, natural chemicals found in grape skins, stems, and seeds, than white wines. But in fact red wines aren't for everyone. All reds—other than Pinot Noir—contain a type of pigment that can (rarely) give some people sinus reactions or headaches. Histamines, found in the skins of red grapes, are also involved in rare allergic reactions.

I think when it comes to wine and health, the best advice is to learn to drink wisely. One of the tricky things about wine and other alcohol consumption is figuring out what is a healthy amount. Medical studies show that one glass or drink a day for women and two for men is better than going without most of the week, then bingeing on five or six drinks in one night. One drink means four to five ounces of wine. Drinking too much on a regular basis can sometimes produce adverse health effects, particularly liver damage. Some studies have also suggested a link between over-consumption of wine and breast cancer in women.

There is a strong tradition of wineries and vintners being involved in philanthropy. Millions of dollars have been raised at many an annual high-profile wine auction, such as the Hospice de Beaune in Burgundy, France, or the Napa Valley Wine Auction in California, with the proceeds going to local hospitals, children's charities, or health clinics that serve low-income people. What's behind the demand for wine at charity auctions? Besides the philanthropic aspect, it may be the mystique and status attached to valuable and rare wines and the auction lots that go with them, such as vacations or access to celebrities. These auctions have offered lots such as dinner with Sophia Loren or a fox-fur hat that once belonged to Marilyn Monroe. In 2000, the highest price ever paid at a charity wine auction was raised for a single bottle of wine: $500,000. A California computer company founder paid the half-million dollars for a six-liter bottle of 1992 Screaming Eagle, a Cabernet Sauvignon from a small winery in the Napa Valley, at the 2000 Napa Valley Wine auction. The overall take from the three-day Napa Valley Wine auction that year was $9.5 million, also a world record for a charity wine auction.

# chapter 2

# when you're out and about

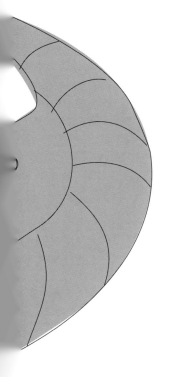

Ordering wine when you're with other people can be quite an unnerving experience. You don't want to look like a complete wine illiterate, but at the same time, you want to enjoy a really nice bottle. So how can you tell which is the perfect wine for you from all those choices on the wine list? And what do the names mean, anyway? Don't panic! There are strategies to ensure that you get something that will be just to your taste. If the restaurant has a *sommelier* (a specialist wine waiter) you're in luck. He or she will certainly have in-depth knowledge of the wines that are on offer. Calling upon this expertise makes great sense—but to get the most from it, it's useful to have an overall idea of what to expect from a wide range of wines. Then you can express your wishes and preferences with greater confidence and clarity. And if you're not happy with your wine, it's essential to know whether you have a good reason for sending the bottle back.

### Ask and you shall receive

Ask questions. That's what *sommeliers* and even regular waiters are there for. You don't need to know wine names or how to pronounce long foreign words; simply describe what you like (red, white, sparkling, or rosé; light, sheer flavors or deep, bold ones) and ask to be steered in the right direction. Then, ask for tastes. Can't decide between the rosé and the Muscadet? Never had a Syrah/Pinot Noir blend before? Ask to try all three. In both restaurants and retail stores, it is often possible to get small tastes of wine, and this is by far the best way to "preview" a wine. After all, someone else's "sheer and light" might be "bold and deep" to you.

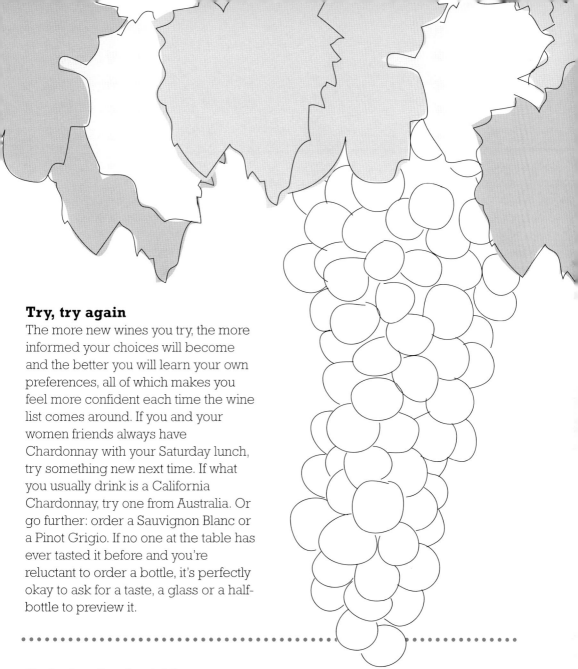

## Try, try again

The more new wines you try, the more informed your choices will become and the better you will learn your own preferences, all of which makes you feel more confident each time the wine list comes around. If you and your women friends always have Chardonnay with your Saturday lunch, try something new next time. If what you usually drink is a California Chardonnay, try one from Australia. Or go further: order a Sauvignon Blanc or a Pinot Grigio. If no one at the table has ever tasted it before and you're reluctant to order a bottle, it's perfectly okay to ask for a taste, a glass or a half-bottle to preview it.

## Ordering for the table

If your companions are shy about it, order for the table. Try to find out what your friends or business associates plan to order and ask them if they usually prefer red or white wines. Often, there will be mixed preferences, and, if so, a light-bodied red, such as Pinot Noir, or a heavier white, such as Viognier or an oaky Chardonnay, will do the trick. Half-bottles or half-carafes of several wines are also a good idea. Think about a half-bottle per person if your companions are wine-lovers and are drinking moderately, less if it's midday or if other activities are on the agenda after the meal.

## What is a *sommelier?*

Sommelier (pronounced "som-el-yay") is a French word for wine server, cellarmaster, or someone in charge of wine. The tradition of having a particular person to choose, stock, serve, and advise about wines originated in France. Historically, the job has been a male province, but today, with the emergence of more women as wine experts, many sommeliers are female. In fact, it's a profession that is attracting growing numbers of wine enthusiasts of both sexes. Someone who has passed a rigorous set of exams, including many blind wine tastings, is a "Master Sommelier," a title conferred by the British Court of Master Sommeliers. Sommeliers not only serve the wine, but they also buy it for the restaurant, so they should be knowledgeable about the wine list. A sommelier is also sometimes called a wine director, wine waiter, or wine steward.

## How to use a *sommelier*

Again, ask questions. If the restaurant you are in has a sommelier, this shows that the management is serious about wine and their wine list. Ask for the wine steward or sommelier if the waiter does not seem knowledgeable about the wines you are interested in. Ask him or her to make suggestions based on wines you like and on what you plan to order for your meal. Generally, you do not have to tip them. They are salaried employees and sometimes receive a commission on the wine they sell. If a wine steward has recommended something you absolutely love and never would have tried if not for her suggestion, a good tip would be ten percent of the bottle price.

## The ABCs of reading a wine list

A wine list can be presented in various ways, often depending upon the way the sommelier has organized it. For instance, it can be divided very simply into red and white wines, or can be listed according to the grape variety used (such as Merlot or Chardonnay), by the wine regions where the wine originates (such as Burgundy or Oregon), or by prices. A good wine list will offer wines in several price tiers, so you can indicate to the waiter or sommelier how much you'd like to spend if that is an issue. Good wine lists include well-known producers and wine regions so diners can recognize wine they have drunk and enjoyed—or not enjoyed—in the past. But better, more exciting wine lists will also have some maverick wine producers, emerging wine areas, or new grape varieties represented so everyone can be pleased, from the tradition-bound to the adventurous.

## A progressive wine list

This type of wine list divides wines into categories according to flavor profiles. There may be a category for "Light, Dry White Wines" and another for "Medium to Full-Bodied Oak-Aged White Wines." Each category of red, white, and sparkling wine begins with lighter wines and progresses to heavier ones. This type of wine list is meant to help people who are not sure of their taste preferences or are not sure what wines match their preferences. It can also be helpful in ordering food to accompany wine because, generally, a "Light, Dry White" wine would best match light cuisine and a "Full-Bodied Red" wine would match heartier fare. (See Chapter 9 for details on pairing food with wine.)

## Take flight

Some restaurants or bars in large cities or wine country regions have flights of wine listed on their menus. A flight is a coordinated series of three or more different, but related, wines served side by side in smaller amounts than a usual glass, but larger than a simple taste. There may be a flight of rosés, two from different regions of France and one from California. Or the flight might be three Tempranillos, all from Spain and from the same vintage, but from three different Spanish wineries. Another popular idea is the same burgundy from the same producer, but three different years (or vintages). The best way to learn about wines is to taste them side by side, so flights are not only fun, they are a great source of education.

## And now <drumroll> the bottle

The person who orders the wine (you) is usually presented with the bottle. Sometimes there is a little fanfare in the gesture. This is often intimidating to people, but calls for nothing more than reading the label to make sure that it is the wine that you ordered. Look not only for the name of the winery and wine type (Chardonnay, Pinot Gris, etc.) but also for the same vintage, or year, that you ordered. It may seem like a small detail, but in some wine-growing regions with variable weather—Oregon, say, more than California—the vintage can make a really big difference to the quality of a wine. How do you know one vintage from another? You don't. That's what your server or sommelier is there for.

## A little taste

The server should always open the bottle at the table—not bring out an open bottle. When the cork is pulled out, it may be handed to you so you can make sure it bears the same markings of the wine producer. There's no need to smell the cork as you can tell much more about a wine from its aroma in the glass. Your server should pour a small amount of wine for you to smell and taste. If all eyes are on you, don't worry; simply act like a pro. Hold the glass by the stem, swirl the wine around in the glass a few times to release the aromas, bring the glass to your nose and sniff. Then taste. When you do, swish the wine around a little in your mouth, almost as if it were mouthwash (but hold the sound effects). The majority of the time, the wine will be fine. Indicate this to the server so he or she can pour for the table.

We've all had to face the challenge of sending a wine back, and it can be nerve-wracking. But there are rules about this! A wine may be "corked," oxidized or bad because of poor storage conditions. This is when you send it back—not because you've changed your mind and now want a red instead of a white, or because you simply don't like the taste of the wine. How to tell whether a wine has turned bad or is simply not to your liking? If a white wine looks honey-colored or a red wine is brownish, they may have oxidized and are no longer good. If there is a musty, wet cardboard smell to the wine, it has been tainted by a bad cork with mold growing in it. If a wine has been improperly stored in temperatures either too cold or too hot, or a bottle has been open for several days before you ordered it by the glass, it will taste "off," and you have a right to send it back.

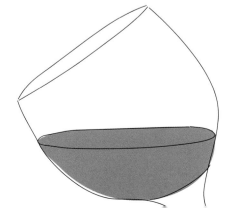

### When you don't like it

There is one instance in which you are justified in rejecting a bottle of wine even when you don't think it is flawed. That is when you have conferred with the sommelier before ordering and he or she recommends and brings you a wine that you told her you would not like. For example, if you clearly stated that you would not like a buttery, heavily oaked Chardonnay and you are brought a bottle that is oily, rich and oak-tasting, tell the wine steward it is exactly what you said you did not like, and ask him/her to find something else. If it is the opposite of what you discussed in advance, you should feel comfortable saying so.

### How to return a flawed bottle gracefully

If you suspect a bottle of wine is tainted, but don't feel confident about your feelings, don't suffer in silence. Ask the sommelier to taste it for you and tell him it doesn't taste right to you. Be as specific as you can. Tell him it smells or tastes moldy, like Brie cheese, or like a barnyard, if that is what you think. Most wine stewards in top restaurants say they take wine back without a fight because they do not want their customers to have a negative dining experience. No matter how it turns out, it will be a learning experience for you.

### New glasses for different wines?

If you are drinking several wines with your dinner, such as a white with your first course of oysters and a red with your main course of baked salmon, do you ask for new wine glasses when the wine is changed? Yes, though you should not have to. A good server will bring fresh glasses with every change of wine. If you order a second or third bottle of the same wine for the table, that is different. If the wine stays the same, the glasses will, too. Feel free, however, to ask for a new glass if the one you have been using has become smudged by your own hands or smells "off."

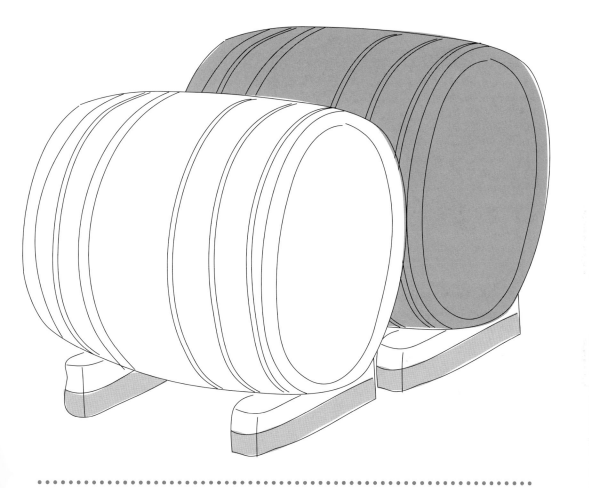

## What to look for in a wine: enjoyment

Wine experts say wines are good when they are "ripe," "balanced," and "well-focused," with "long, lingering aftertastes." They are bad when they lack these things and when their "tannins," "acidity" or "oak flavors" dominate the wine. But what do these words mean to you? (See Chapter 6 for a glossary of common wine terms.) If they mean nothing, then throw them out!

What counts most of all is your own pleasure, and just as a fingerprint and a zebra's stripes are unique, so is every set of taste buds. You may enjoy what your spouse finds too sweet, too strong or boring. But just as you don't feel embarrassed or "uneducated" because you don't like Gorgonzola cheese or lamb, you should not feel deficient if you don't also like the dense, chewy Zinfandel or crisp Sauvignon Blanc your friends are raving about.

## What to expect from:

### Barbera

Sometimes called "the people's wine" of Piedmont, the wine region in northwest Italy whence the Barbera grape hails, this wine competes with Sangiovese as Italy's most common and popular red wine. The wine will usually be crisp and easy to drink, not dense and chewy. A Barbera should have a deep ruby color, berry flavors, a medium body, refreshing acidity, and low tannin levels (tannins are those things that make your mouth pucker). Drink it with or without food, and take it along or order it anywhere from a formal dinner party to a summer picnic.

### A Bordeaux blend

This wine is what has given the preeminent red-wine region in the world, the Bordeaux area of France, its classy reputation. These are dense red wines that are usually a blend of Cabernet Sauvignon, Cabernet Franc, and Merlot. They are known for their finesse and high quality, and are among the most expensive wines in the world. They are perhaps most valued for their longevity, so if you see such a wine and it is older than anything else on the wine list, don't be put off. The wine is also sometimes called a "claret."

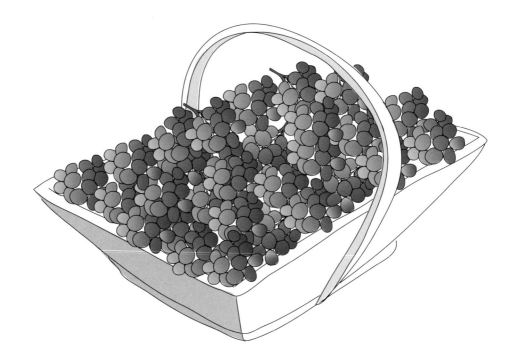

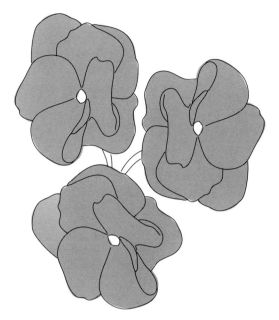

## Cabernet Franc

Native to Bordeaux, this is a dry, red wine, often a part of a Bordeaux blend (along with Cabernet Sauvignon and Merlot) but it can also stand alone. A fleshy, full-flavored, 100 percent Cabernet Franc can simply be too powerful for some people. The wine boasts a blood-red color with possible aromas of pine needles, dried grass, and crushed violets. Expect a velvety texture and flavors of burnt caramel, cherry or cranberry. Drink this wine with hearty grilled meats and vegetables. As the basis for a dry rosé wine, Cabernet Franc can provide fresh strawberry flavors.

## Cabernet Sauvignon

This dry red wine comes from the king of French wine grapes, the Cabernet Sauvignon. It can range from opulent, as in many Napa Valley versions, to elegant and smooth, as in French versions. Good Cabernets can also come from Chile, Australia, and Argentina. Most are finely made and highly priced, but there is no shortage; it is among the most widely planted wine grape varieties in the world. Expect intense, dark-fruit flavors (such as black cherry, blackberry, and cassis) and fruity aromas. This is a wine that ages well; it should not be drunk too young. Drink alone or with grilled red meats, sausages or strong cheeses. Many wineries make wines that are 100 percent Cabernet, but many others blend in small amounts of Merlot or Cabernet Franc.

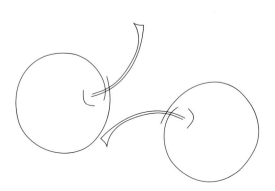

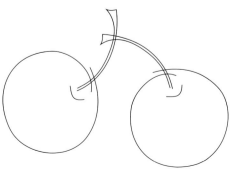

## Carmenère

This is a deeply colored, full-bodied, dry, and sometimes powerful red wine that comes mainly from Chile, where until recently it was often confused with Merlot in the vineyards. It is sometimes blended with Cabernet Sauvignon and sometimes stands on its own. The grape, originally used in France, is becoming the emblematic grape of Chile, where the climate and soils of its northern wine producing valleys are ideal for growing it. Expect aromas of spice, jam, raspberry, and dark chocolate, and flavors of tobacco, fig, and chocolate. Drink with hearty dishes containing red meats, beans, robust pasta sauces, and grilled red meats.

## Champagne

Sparkling wine from Champagne, France, will almost always be a blend of Chardonnay, Pinot Noir, and Pinot Meunier. In deference to the area where the champagne method was invented, most producers outside Champagne who make the same beverage call theirs "sparkling wine." Under French law, winemakers outside the Champagne region are prohibited from using the word "Champagne" on their labels, but few non-European producers feel bound by this. Sparkling wines are not inferior to Champagne, they merely come from another region. Expect a pale-straw (or pale-salmon color if it is a rosé Champagne) and flavors of strawberry, redcurrants, nutmeg, spice, peach, blackberry, apple or pear. Many Champagnes are dry (brut), delicate, and crisp, but some are creamier and sweeter. Don't save Champagne or sparkling wine for caviar or wedding cake; drink it with mussels, oysters, wild mushrooms, roasted chicken, and roast pork tenderloin.

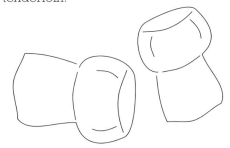

## Chardonnay

This grape hails from the Burgundy region of France and is wildly popular in the United States. Because it grows well in a variety of climates and sites, there are good Chardonnays from almost all wine regions of the world, especially (if you prefer the full-bodied type) California and Australia. The aroma of the wine can sometimes be buttery. The flavor varies according to where it's grown and the style of the winemaker—it can range from clean, crisp, and minerally (as in fine Chablis) to fruity, rich, and toasty if it has been aged in oak barrels. From most Chardonnays, expect flavors of apple, mango, pear, pineapple, lemon, fig, peach, and honey. Drink alone or with grilled chicken, salmon, shrimp, crab, lobster, light pasta, and lightly spiced foods.

## Chenin Blanc

Most often from the Loire in France, California or South Africa, this is usually a soft, off-dry (slightly sweet) white wine made from the Chenin Blanc grape. If French, the bottle could say Vouvray, Montlouis or Savennières, the specific wine regions the wine comes from. A Chenin Blanc can also be a very sweet dessert wine, as it is a grape that can be made in several different styles, so be sure to ask before ordering. In a dinner wine, expect a pleasantly fruity, clean wine with flavors of lemon, melon, apple, peach, citrus fruit or chamomile that you can drink with the spiciest of ethnic foods.

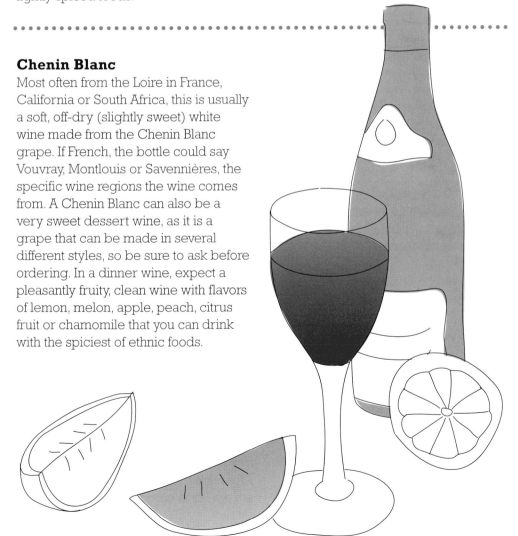

### Gewürztraminer

The German word Gewürz means "spice," and indicates the flowery and spicy aromas and flavors of this wine. If you're in a "spicy" mood, try this wine! It can be made in a range of styles from sweet to dry, so make sure the description indicates this or ask your server. Good Gewürztraminer comes from France, Germany, California, Chile, and other places. Expect aromas of cinnamon, clove, citrus, peach or apricot. The wine is often recommended as a companion to spicy foods, such as Thai and Indian.

### Grenache

Widespread in the Rhône region of France, this fruity red wine is gaining popularity in the United States and Australia. In Spain it is called Garnacha, and in Rioja, it is second in importance to the famous Tempranillo. It is often blended with other red grapes, such as Syrah and Cabernet Sauvignon. If the wine is French, some of the best examples will be from Châteauneuf-du-Pape or Gigondas. You can expect full, concentrated, wines with aromas of minerals, wet earth, and plums, and flavors that hint of leather, prunes, and roasted chestnuts. Drink this wine with hearty foods, including red meats, and strong cheeses.

### Malbec

A dry, red wine originally used as a blending grape in Bordeaux. Today it is the star grape of Argentina's emerging wine industry and is often grown in that country's high-altitude vineyards. There are also Malbecs or Malbec blends from neighboring Chile. Expect juicy, deep, fruit flavors, such as raspberry, with hints of coffee, and cinnamon, along with a lot of tannin. This can be a chewy wine. Drink with grilled red meats, chicken, blood sausages, and even goat, as they would at an Argentine barbecue. Argentine wines are a relative bargain around the world.

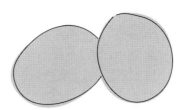

## Merlot

This soft, fruity red wine is popular with consumers as an approachable alternative to Cabernet Sauvignon. Grown and made throughout the world, it is widely used in Bordeaux, France. Expect smooth, fruit flavors of red and black cherry, berry, plum, and redcurrant with hints of spice, tobacco, and licorice. The aromas and flavors of Merlot can vary widely from vineyard to vineyard and bottle to bottle, so don't expect one to taste exactly like the last Merlot you had. Drink with grilled red meats, hamburgers, tuna and swordfish, pizzas, and stews. Merlot is often consumed younger than most Cabernets.

## Muscadet

This dry, clean-tasting white wine comes from the Loire region of France. Expect a sheer white wine with crisp, light flavors of lemon, apple, pear, grapefruit, minerals, and herbs. Ideally drunk with oysters and other light seafood dishes.

## Nebbiolo

This is usually a powerhouse of a dry, red wine. In Italy, premium wines made from the Nebbiolo grape are considered on a par with the finest French burgundies. It's the leading grape from Piedmont, Italy, and goes into two of its best known products, Barolo and Barbaresco. When grown in California, where it does well in the cooler, northern part of the state, the bottle will usually say Nebbiolo on it. Expect flavors of cherry, roses, tobacco, tar, cinnamon, and chocolate truffles. Drink with hearty, stick-to-your-ribs dishes, and grilled meats.

## Pinot Grigio

This is a popular dry white wine made chiefly in Italy, France, Germany, Austria, and Oregon (where it is called Pinot Gris). Pinot Grigio is the top imported wine in the United States and its popularity is already beginning to rival that of Chardonnay. Expect rich, spicy, tropical-fruit aromas and flavors in a Pinot Gris from France and a delicate, light, crisp wine with citrus-fruit flavors from Italian versions. Pinot Grigio is usually a modestly priced wine. Drink with lighter cuisine such as seafood and delicately sauced vegetable or chicken dishes.

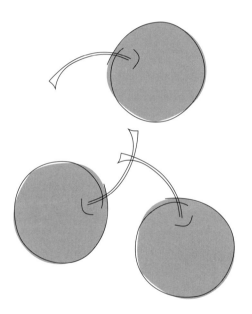

## Pinot Noir

The fragile, finicky Pinot Noir grape is temperamental—on the one hand it can can produce some of the world's most collectible wines, on the other, a thin "breakfast wine" without much life to it. Look for higher-priced Pinot Noirs from Burgundy, Oregon or the Russian River Valley of California. Expect sumptuous velvety textures, and flavors and aromas of red cherry, raspberry, raisins, violets, and earth. Drink young or at five to ten years old at the very most. Pinot Noir is a food-friendly wine to drink with roasted chicken, duck, pork, salmon, and mushrooms.

## Riesling

Consumers still have some misconceptions about Rieslings because they assume they are all sweet wines that don't go with food. But the best Rieslings are dry wines, such as the steely, aromatic Riesling Kabinetts from Germany. Increasingly, Riesling is being grown in many other parts of the world. Styles range from dry to semi-sweet and super-sweet in dessert wines. Expect delicate floral aromas such as jasmine, rose, or orange blossom and flavors of honeysuckle, nectarine, peach, tangerine, and minerals. Drink with spicy foods, shellfish, curries, chicken, veal, pork, and summer salads.

## Sangiovese

The star grape of Tuscany, perhaps the most idyllic wine region of Italy, Sangiovese produces a dry red wine. Some Sangiovese also comes from California, made by Italian immigrants who want to revive a wine tradition from their homeland. This is the grape that plays a large role in Chianti, the wine in the basket-wrapped bottle. Newer versions from both Tuscany and California now have world-class status. Expect a deep-colored wine that is lighter in texture and flavor than a Cabernet Sauvignon with flavors of red fruit. Sangiovese can also be blended with Cabernet Sauvignon or Merlot in a "Super-Tuscan" wine. Drink with pizza, strongly flavored pasta dishes, grilled meats, and sauced vegetable dishes.

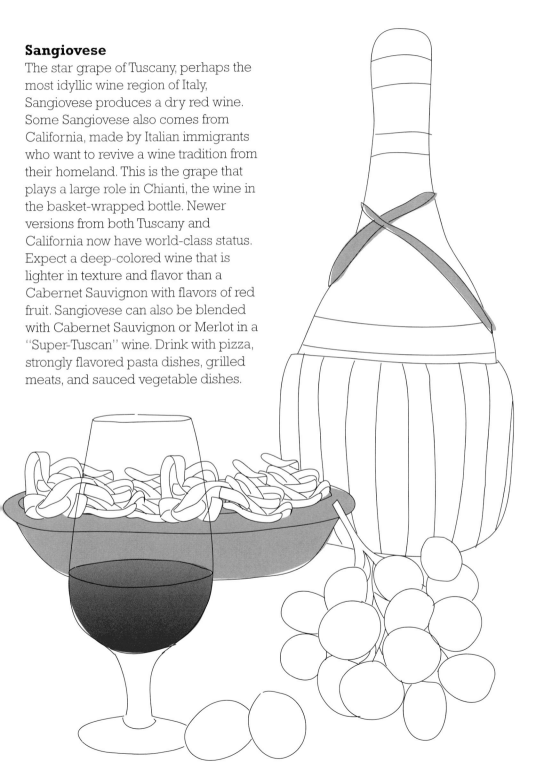

### Sauvignon Blanc (also called Fumé Blanc)

This is a crisp, dry white wine that originally comes from France but is made in many countries today; New Zealand is the main player in the New World, while Chile is producing impressive examples. Expect aromas and flavors of lemon, pear, melon, apple, grapefruit, hay or grass. Drink it with light cuisine such as shellfish, sole, halibut, chicken, salads, vegetables, and citrus-fruit sauces. Sauvignon Blanc can also be a very sweet dessert wine similar to Sauternes.

### Syrah (also called Shiraz in Australia)

Syrah is originally from the Rhône area of France, but is also grown in many parts of the United States and has become one of Australia's star wines. Expect a spicy, full-flavored wine with aromas and flavors of blackberry, cherry, sage, and leather. The wine is best drunk not too young as it needs time to age and smooth out. Drink with grilled red meats, wild game, and stews. There is no relation between Syrah and the wine known as Petite Sirah.

### Tempranillo

This dry red is the king of Spanish wines. Though it often stands alone, it can also be blended with other grapes, such as Grenache. It is typically an elegant wine, with concentrated, dark-fruit flavors, that ages very well. In fact, some are not made to drink young, so don't be afraid to order ones that have been in the bottle for several years. Expect aromas of fruit jam and tastes of smoke, pepper, and other spices such as clove and cinnamon. Drink with grilled meats, strong cheese, and strongly flavored vegetable dishes with spicy sauces.

## White Zinfandel

This is a soft, white wine made from the hearty red Zinfandel grape. Called a "blush" wine because of its pretty pink color, this fruity wine was invented in the Napa Valley in the 1970s and became so popular it is often credited with boosting wine consumption in the United States. The blush color is achieved by removing the red skins from the grape pulp and juice within a few hours of crushing so that the juice's tint is light rather than a deep red color. Expect a somewhat sweet wine, with aromas of strawberries and watermelon, that goes down easily and complements many foods, especially those with some heat such as Asian or Latin cuisine.

Have you discovered the enticing charms of Viognier? If not, you have a treat in store. This is a great wine to order if you're looking for a Chardonnay alternative (you must have heard of the "ABC"—Anything But Chardonnay—movement?). Originally from the Rhône area of France and made also in various parts of California, Viognier is a stylish, full-bodied, dry white wine with a touch of the spiciness of a Gewürztraminer. Expect flavors of honeysuckle, peach, citrus fruit, minerals, and apricot. Drink it to accompany light snacks such as olives or raw vegetables, or with light cuisine, such as seafood, chicken and pork with light sauces.

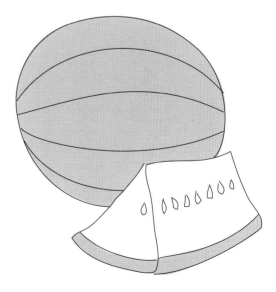

## Zinfandel

Often called the most American of wine grapes and a popular favorite at the Thanksgiving holiday meal, Zinfandel is chiefly cultivated in California. Though it was once thought to have descended from Italy's Primitivo grape, recent research at the University of California, Davis, has traced its roots back to Croatia (see Chapter 9 for further details). Expect a bold, red wine with aromas of black pepper and flavors of cranberry, plum, raisin, raspberry, red cherry, and boysenberry. Don't drink it too young, as the dry style of this wine needs aging to settle its acidity. Drink Zinfandel with sausages, ribs, beef, tomato sauces, pizza, Cajun dishes, and grilled vegetables.

## How much will I pay in a restaurant?

Everybody's got to make a living, and most restaurants make theirs by doubling or even tripling the wholesale price they pay for wines they will serve you. A $10 wine at wholesale becomes a $20 to $30 wine on a restaurant wine list—sometimes even more. Restaurants make even more money selling wine by the glass. Destination restaurants sometimes charge for a glass what they paid for the whole bottle (a bottle holds about 4.5 glasses). Many wine consumers object to this and even boycott restaurants that mark up the price of a wine too much. Restaurants defend this practice by saying they make most of their profits on wine and other alcoholic drinks because the preparation of food is so labor-intensive.

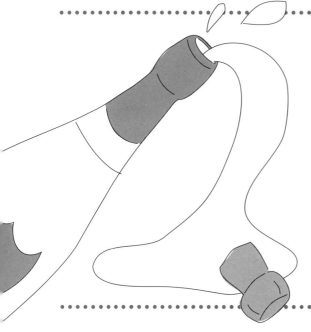

## Don't be afraid to be cheap!

At least once in your life (and maybe more often) order the cheapest bottle of wine on the menu. Especially in a "good" restaurant, you will often get a treat—a delicious wine at a value price. Wine buyers at restaurants often report that they seldom have a hard time unloading the most expensive wines on their lists, but have much more difficulty selling wines at the other end of the scale. At the same time, they say they would not have the wine on their list if it wasn't good!

## What is a corkage fee?

"Corkage" or a "corkage fee" is what a restaurant charges you to open and serve a bottle of wine that you bring into the restaurant. In some places, the laws may forbid it. But where it is allowed, some restaurants may charge no corkage fee, some charge it to most customers but not local residents, and some charge outrageous fees all the time to anyone, so be sure to call ahead and ask what a restaurant's policy is before you tote along a special bottle. You should not bring a bottle that is on the restaurant's wine list. Most restaurants will uphold a corkage fee policy because they generally want to discourage the practice of diners bringing their own wine (see above).

## Can you take leftover wine home?

Whether it's the wine they've brought to the restaurant or wine they have purchased from the restaurant's own wine list, some people may like to take the wine they have not finished home with them, especially when there is a considerable amount left in the bottle. This is not always legal, so it is always best ask to check with your server or sommelier. In general, though, this is not a common practice.

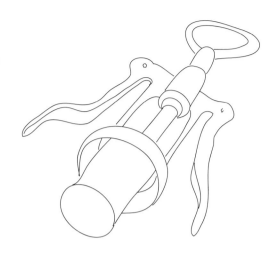

## Why pay for corkage?

Paying a $10 to $15 corkage fee seems reasonable to some people who would otherwise pay $35 for a wine on a restaurant's list, especially when they got that special bottle of wine on sale or as a gift. Others would rather bring a favorite wine they know than take a chance—sometimes be an expensive chance—on wines they've never tried or heard of. But why would someone take a top-price bottle of wine along to a top-flight restaurant and then pay a $50 corkage fee? Well, you'd have to ask them…

when you're out and about

## Can you say...?

One of the most often cited reasons for the lack of popularity of some wines, especially German, French, and Italian, is that people are intimidated to order them because they don't know how to pronounce their names! Here are some tongue twisters that you should not hesitate to try:

**Gewürztraminer** (German)—Ga-VURTZ-tra-mee-ner
**Viognier** (French)—VEE-oh-nyay
**Sauvignon Blanc** (French)—Sow-vee-nyawn-BLAWNK
**Pinot Noir** (French)—PEE-no Nwhar
**Muscadet** (French)—Mus-ka-DAY
**Pinot Grigio** (Italian)—PEE-no GREE-joe
**Sangiovese** (Italian)—San-joe-VAY-zee
**Nebbiolo** (Italian)—Neb-ee-OH-lo
**Tempranillo** (Spanish)—Tem-pra-NEE-yo
**Claret** (British English)—cla-ret: the "a" is pronounced like the "a" in "cat, and the "et" as in "forget".

### wine buff

Ever wonder why the American wine industry embraced tasting rooms so warmly? Wine was hard to sell after the thirteen-year period of Prohibition (1920–1933), when alcoholic beverages were illegal in America. Also, wine was unfamiliar to those who did not grow up in wine-drinking families. From the tasting room's origins —in Sonoma County in 1943 and the Napa Valley in 1956—has grown a firm U.S. tradition of opening a winery's door to the public for free tastes of wine and tours of the facility. These visits provide lifetime memories for tourists—ones they do not forget the next time they see a wine on the shelf at the market. Winery owners believe these can create a loyal customer base, and so they happily give out samples of their wine, often with such nibbles as cheese, fruit, chocolates, and salty snacks.

# chapter 3

# how to
# buy wine

When you know what you like to drink, buying wine can be a delightfully absorbing and pleasurable experience. On the other hand, if you're not at all wine savvy, and don't know one bottle from another, it can be a tense nightmare. Decisions, decisions. How to decide from among all those names and places? Faced with an array of bottles, it's tempting to pick up the nearest one, hand over your money at the checkout, and get out of there. But that way you'd be missing so much. You need a strategy: so be utterly shameless—confess to everyone—friends, wine waiters, clerks at wine stores, that you would like help and advice about buying wine. You'll be amazed at how willing people are to impart their knowledge. The owner of your small local wine shop will be a mine of information—with more time to talk to you, and get to know your likes and dislikes. As for worrying about how much to spend, set a realistic amount that you can afford. You'll discover excellent, drinkable wines in your price range.

## Rely on sales help

Don't be shy! Ask for a knowledgeable salesperson and shop only at stores with staff trained to help customers make decisions. Most quality wine shops offer this service, and a growing number of supermarkets and upscale groceries do also. These people are familiar with the wines they sell and can steer you in the right direction once they know your preferences, your budget, and the occasion you're buying for, whether it's a special anniversary or a rainy-night dinner at home.

## What is your "style?"

Just as different people have certain styles, so does wine. When you walk into a retail store and ask a salesperson for help, one of the first questions you're likely to be asked is what type of wine you like. Often, it is not enough to say "white," or even "Chardonnay." Many French Chardonnays can be crisp and lean; those from California can be buttery and oak-tasting; and in yet another style, those from Australia can be oily, fruity powerhouses of flavor. If your preferences lie with one of these styles, it would be a disappointment to get one of the others. So think about wine style as a starting point to buying wines you will enjoy.

## Take care

Make sure you buy wine on a regular basis from stores that take proper care of their inventory. Direct sunlight, extreme heat or cold, and dramatic temperature fluctuations can ruin wine before it is even opened. If you notice any of these conditions when you're inside the store, look for another place to purchase your wine. In any specific bottle, make sure while you are in the store that the liquid in the bottle reaches its neck, that the cork is not pushing out of the bottle, and that there are no signs of leakage.

## Taste, if you can

Many fine-wine shops offer wine tasting, so you can sample before buying. Some shops will schedule their wine tasting on a certain day at a certain time, so ask about your shop's schedule. There is no better way to tell if you will enjoy a new wine. Talk to the salespeople who are pouring. Ask what they taste in the wine you are trying and see if you also taste the cassis or black pepper that they noted. You're not wrong if you don't; trying wines this way is simply part of your education. In these free tastings, expose yourself to new wines you would hesitate to order in a restaurant.

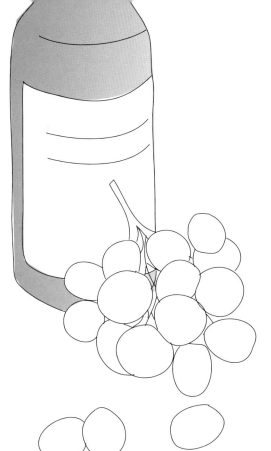

## Where should I shop?

Fine-wine shop in the best part of town? Discount beverage warehouse on the wrong side of the tracks? What is the best place to buy your wine? Look for a store that is service-oriented, one that will try to determine its customers' preferences over a period of time through interaction into the types of foods they enjoy, the grape varieties they prefer, and the people they socialize with. This may mean a small shop in your area, but it may mean a larger store, too. Look for stores that have been around a long time; that indicates they're good at what they do. When you develop a relationship with a favorite retailer, let them understand you and your tastes better by giving them feedback after you drink the wines they have sold you.

## Wine clubs

In the age of high technology, you can also shop for wine with your computer or by telephone. Wine clubs, prevalent in the United States and Australia, are increasing in popularity and are a convenient way to shop for yourself or give gifts to the wine-lovers in your life. Wine clubs are usually sponsored by wineries, which sell only their own wines, plus gifts and memorabilia from their winery retail stores. Wine club memberships can vary from one to twelve months, and depending on the winery, they can vary quite a bit in price, but all wines are discounted to members. Shipping can be tricky because of interstate shipping laws involving alcohol, so make sure you visit the web site (or call the toll free number) of the winery you are interested in to determine if they can ship to you. Most U.S. wineries can ship to at least a dozen states, some many more. The clubs can also be separate commercial enterprises not affiliated with any one winery. A caveat: Some wine retailers say that wine clubs are often clearing houses for well-known producers to quickly sell off inferior vintages.

## How much should I expect to pay in a store?

Traditional mark-ups on wines for retail stores, such as your corner fine wine shop, are fifty percent over the wholesale price the store pays to a distributor. So a bottle that costs the retail shop $10 will be marked up to $15 on the retail shelf. There are exceptions; some retailers offer discounts because they get discounts on volume purchases, so watch for bins laden with specials. But with so many good wines being made and exported from Europe, California, Chile, Argentina, South Africa, New Zealand, and Australia, you need not spend a lot of money to get your wine education going or even to deepen it.

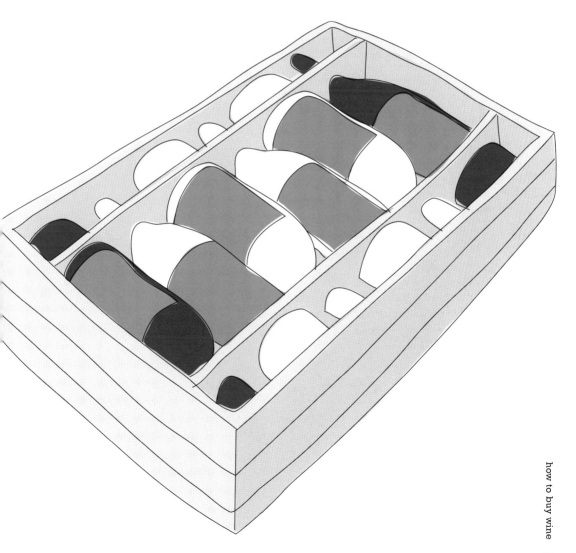

## Should you buy at the winery?

In terms of price, the winery is often the worse place to shop because most wineries do not have sales. They offer their wines at suggested retail prices because they know most people visiting the winery are on vacation and in the mood to spend money! That's why so many retail shops at wineries these days contain not only the wines they produce but gifts, food, wine paraphernalia, and even clothes. But many wineries make small-production wines that never go into retail stores and are available only at the winery. If you taste such a wine and like it, you may well wish to buy some even if it's not bargained-priced.

Why are some wines so expensive? We all ask this question from time to time—I know I have. Sometimes, the answer is simply scarcity—often, small supply equals big demand. Some of the most desirable wines in the marketplace (and hence the most expensive) are the so-called "cult" or "boutique" wines in California (such winemakers are known as *garagistes* in Europe). These are wines made in extremely small amounts because there is no big winery behind them—some are literally made in garages or warehouses. Others may be made at a "custom crush" facility that rents out its equipment and space for the winemaking process. Of course, this usually also means such wines are handcrafted with much attention to detail, so they can be very special.

## Cheaper by the dozen

Most retail stores will offer discounts of ten to fifteen percent on purchases of twelve or more bottles so when you discover a wine you especially like, consider buying it by the case, which is usually twelve bottles (for extremely limited production wines, a case may be six bottles). High-quality wines of limited production can be purchased based on the vintage. Wines of "good"

quality, but made in quantities larger than 2,000 to 3,000 cases are often blended and bottled as needed. So if you find a particularly good 2002 Sauvignon Blanc from a California winery and wish to purchase a case of it, ask your salesperson to check the lot number or bottling date on the box. By doing so you can be reasonably sure that the glass you had last night will be the same wine you buy today.

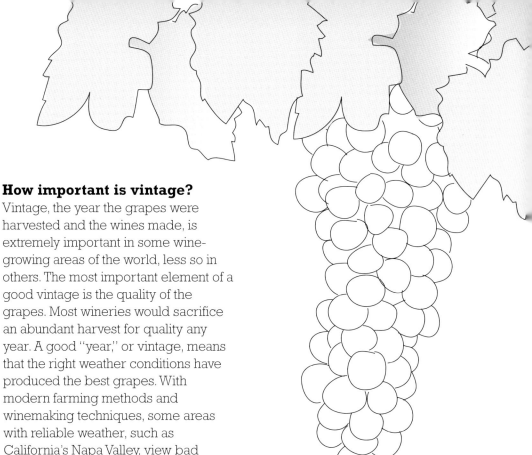

## How important is vintage?

Vintage, the year the grapes were harvested and the wines made, is extremely important in some wine-growing areas of the world, less so in others. The most important element of a good vintage is the quality of the grapes. Most wineries would sacrifice an abundant harvest for quality any year. A good "year," or vintage, means that the right weather conditions have produced the best grapes. With modern farming methods and winemaking techniques, some areas with reliable weather, such as California's Napa Valley, view bad harvests as a thing of the past. That does not mean there won't be differences in each vintage, but there will be very few vintages that bomb completely. In other areas, such as Bordeaux or rainy Oregon, the weather is more variable and unpredictable. So, too, is the quality of the wine produced from year to year.

## What about bottles?

Port bottles are shaped differently than Bordeaux bottles, which are different from burgundy bottles, which are different from sparkling-wine bottles. Does it matter? Shape of the bottle is founded mostly on the traditions of a region or industry and usually does not change. Probably the single most important factor in a bottle's shape is that it lends itself to being laid on its side for storage to keep the cork moist. Some producers will not put their wines in clear glass because they believe that exposure to light could harm the wine, but others prefer clear glass to see the wine's color. Look for browning in older whites and rosés when bottled in clear glass. It is a good indication that the wine is on the downhill side of drinkability.

## Sizing up bottles

The standard size of a wine bottle is 750 milliliters, which yields about 4.5 glasses of wine. Gaining in popularity are 375 milliliter bottles, also called half bottles, because of the flexibility they offer to consumers. Other bottle sizes you may encounter are "splits," used only for Champagne, which hold 187 milliliters of wine (one serving), and large-format bottles such as magnums, which hold 1.5 liters or two standard bottles of wine, and jeroboams, also called three-liter bottles and double magnums. Don't ever try to pour the largest-sized bottle of wine, the Nebuchadnezzar, by yourself—it holds fifteen liters, or twenty standard bottles.

## The dent in the bottom

There's a word for that dent on the bottom of a wine bottle—it's called a punt. It is found on the bottom of Champagne/sparkling-wine bottles and some still wine bottles. The main purpose of the rounded bottom or punt is to strengthen the bottle—especially important for sparkling wines—but punts also can be useful for collecting sediment and some waiters find them handy for pouring wine, since it provides a place to put your thumb.

## What about special gold medal winners?

Do wine knowledge and tasting ability sometimes seem like competitive sports? Well actually they are. Wine competitions are often where vintners try to distinguish themselves in a competitive market. But when you are shopping for wine, should you stop at the bin that says "Gold Medal Winner?" For some people, using medal winners as consumer aids might amount to hand-holding that discourages them from learning their own tastes. For others, especially those uncomfortable with wine, having a gold medal attached to a wine is definitely a recommendation of quality and will encourage them to try something they might not otherwise. You might want to pay attention if a wine does well in numerous competitions.

Should you pay attention to wine writers? Well, I'm always delighted when someone says they like my recommendations! In fact the best strategy is to calibrate your tastes with the writer's. Some wine writers reward wines that are robust, tannic, and filled with character even if the wines may be flawed. They may feel that if a winemaker is willing to walk that tightrope of making "imperfect" wines to offer the consumer a beverage that is full of personality, then "bravo!" Another writer might be more inclined to give higher scores to wines that technically strive for perfection, even if this limits the audience to the fringes of the consumer spectrum. A wine writer may declare he hardly ever drinks white wine, and prefers strong reds. If you prefer white wines, this is hardly helpful, so try to find a critic who seems open-minded and reflects your tastes as closely as possible.

## Can I return a bottle of wine to a store?

Yes, but only when there is something wrong with the wine. It could be "corked," meaning that mold growing in the cork has imparted a moldy taste to the wine, or it could be "oxidized," meaning air has gotten by the cork, turned the wine brownish, and given it a cooked or baked flavor like sherry. Wine-industry insiders say as many as five to ten percent of bottles may be corked. But if you simply do not like the wine inside the bottle, that is not enough reason to return it.

# What to look for in wine labels

### How to read a label in any language

Although they vary in some ways from country to country, most wine labels in most languages will contain the following information: the name of the wine, the vintage year, the estate, *château*, winery or producer that made the wine, a quality designation, the alcohol content, the volume of wine in the bottle, the country of origin, and the more specific appellation, or geographic area, from which the wine hails. A label might also say what specific grape varieties were used for the wine, and whether it is red, white, rosé or sparkling.

Should you judge a wine by its label? No, except when labels are so whimsical or fun that you want the bottle just for the label. Fancy labels and fine packaging are sometimes designed to send a message to the consumer: I look expensive, I am expensive, I am worth it! In medium-priced categories where competition among wines is fiercest, wine producers know that eye-catching, colorful labels are important to attract consumers' attention when their product is on the shelf with hundreds of others. Wines with long, established histories have built their brands over many years and rely on elegant, understated packaging that remains unchanged vintage to vintage.

### Every label tells a story

So, you're in the store surrounded by a dizzying array of bottles. As you browse, you'll probably zero in on a few labels. Wine labels can generally be divided into two types: ones that highlight the grape variety used (Merlot, for example) and others that mention the geographic area in which the wine grapes were grown and/or in which the wine was made. Wines from the United States, Australia, New Zealand, and South America fall into the "grape variety" category. If they contain the name of a grape variety, they must contain at least seventy-five percent of that grape; the rest can be one or two other grape varieties that the winemaker feels balance out the primary one. Here, and on the following pages are some "virtual" wine labels that have been devised to give you an idea of what to look for.

## French wine labels

If you like French wine and plan to buy lots of it, you will want to know a little about how to read wine labels in France. The wine label will generally highlight the sub-region from which the wine comes (such as Pauillac or Margaux, which are both within the Bordeaux region) over the grape variety (such as Chardonnay or Merlot) because the French traditionally exalt place over everything. In fact, in many cases a wine producer is forbidden from putting the name of the grape variety on the label. So you need to learn the prominent varieties in each region. For example, the Sancerre appellation is known primarily for Sauvignon Blanc. A French label may also list the classification of the château or region. For example, the classification premier cru, which means "first growth," refers to the ranking of the vineyard in which the grapes for that particular wine were grown.

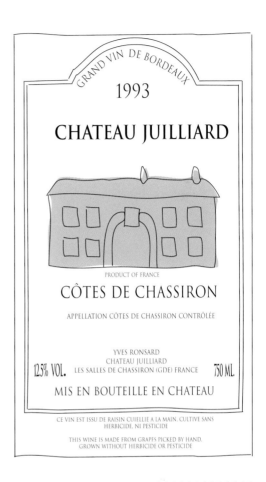

## Italian wine labels

Italian wine labels will often have the name of the grape variety as well as the geographic area where the wine was made, instead of one or the other. For quality assurance, look for the words Denominazione di Origine Controllata e Garantita (DOCG)—this is the highest quality designation in Italy. Vino da tavola indicates everyday table wine. Top wine regions, which may be listed on the front label, include Piedmont and Chianti Classico.

## German wine labels

Many people say the difficulty of reading German wine labels is one of the chief reasons German wines are not drunk more commonly around the world! But if you like the delicacy and versatility of a German Riesling, or the honeyed richness of an Eiswein, don't let the labels put you off. Perhaps the most important thing to zero in on with a German label is its quality category. Qualitätswein mit Prädikat (shortened to QmP) is the highest category of German wine quality, so if your bottle says that, you can be reasonably sure you are getting something worth trying. Tafelwein (table wine) is the lowest quality level of wine, followed by Landwein (which is similar to French vin de pays) but you will probably only encounter these if you are traveling in Germany. Riesling is also the premier grape of Germany, so look for that—particularly if it is a Riesling Kabinett (see below).

## Ripeness

Another designation that can be found on a German wine label refers to the level of grape ripeness that went into the wine. What does this mean, exactly? The ripeness of the grapes when they are picked to make a wine is crucially important because that level indicates whether a wine is light in body (and usually dry and lightweight in flavor) or full and rich (and usually sweeter). There is an ascending hierarchy of these ripeness levels, which are determined mainly (though not exclusively) by the sugar content of the grapes before fermentation. Kabinett is at the light end of the scale, which moves up to Spätlese, Auslese, Beerenauslese, Trockenbeerenauslese, and Eiswein. The first two are generally dry dinner wines that are reasonably priced, while the last four get noticeably sweeter and more expensive as they move up this scale.

S.A.Baum

Weingut Nackenheim in Rhein

1985

Nackenheimer Frühling
Riesling Spätlese

Qualitätswein mit Prädikat

GUTTSHABFÜLLUNG

alc. 11.5% vol.          750 ml.

RHEINHESSEN

GARCIA

*Ribera del Duero*

DENOMINACION DE ORIGIN

CRIANZA 1997

Elaborado y embotellado en la propiedas
BODEGA GARCIA, S.A.
VALBUENA DE DUERO
PRODUCT OF SPAIN

LOTE. Nº 3

750 ML.
ALC 12.5% BY VOL.

## Spanish wine labels

When reading the label of a Spanish wine, look for the chief quality indicator, Denominación de Origen (Denominación de Origen Calificada in the case of Rioja), which indicates that the wine comes from an official wine region and has met certain high standards in the growing of its grapes and the winemaking process. Another quality designation refers to the aging of the wines and the grapes from which they are made. These designations, which are indicated somewhere on the wine label, are crianza, reserva or gran reserva, the last one being the very highest quality level. You should also look on the label for Spain's leading wine regions, such as Rioja, Ribera del Duero or Priorato.

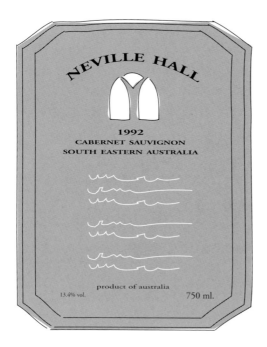

## Australian wine labels

Australia has a long history of winemaking and produces some of the highest quality wines anywhere. Its winemakers are some of the best in the world. Their approach to the rules and laws that govern winemaking is much less tradition-bound than in Europe. So Australian wine labels look much like ones from the United States, and are generally quite clear and unfettered with details. When a grape variety appears on the label, such as Shiraz (the French Syrah), at least eighty-five percent of that grape must be in the bottle. Otherwise, an Australian wine label will list the winery name, alcohol content, vintage, and wine region.

## United States wine labels

America also has a long and proud history of high-quality winemaking. As with Australian wine labels, American labels are refreshingly simple to read and understand. In fact, they are allowed to contain less information than European labels chiefly because there are fewer regulations and laws governing wine. Usually, the label will contain the name of the winery, the grape variety the wine is primarily made from, the area from which it comes, and the alcohol content. But by federal law, American wine labels must also contain a health warning about the dangers of alcohol consumption that is not found on wines produced in the rest of the world.

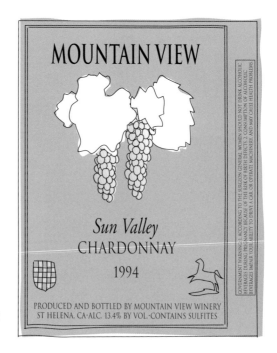

## What does "reserve" mean?

In many European wines, *riserva*, in Italian, or *reserva*, in Spanish, means the wines have been aged longer than those not carrying this moniker. But in the United States, there is no legal meaning attached to the term "Reserve," which you might see on a front label. Wineries usually use it to denote a higher level of quality than wines that do not use it. Sometimes, the term "Reserve" indicates that the wine was made from the finest grapes of the vintage. Expect to pay more for reserve wines.

## What does "vineyard-designated" mean?

According to U.S. law, ninety-five percent of the grapes in a wine must come from one particular vineyard in order for a producer to include the vineyard designation on the label. The label will say something like "Katherine's Vineyard," or "Redhead Vineyard." Wineries will do this, often naming the vineyards after loved ones, to show that the wine in the bottle is not only from a very particular spot, but a particularly esteemed spot that grows the best grapes. You should expect to pay higher prices for wines that mention the specific vineyard from which the grapes originate.

## What does the term "estate-bottled" mean?

You may also find the words "Estate-Bottled" on a bottle of American wine. This means the winery owns and grows the grapes that are in the wine—it's analogous to a restaurant saying its apple pie is "homemade." You may wonder why there is a special term to indicate this, but many wineries do not grow their own grapes, but buy them from grape growers. Some don't even make the wine; they buy finished wine from other producers, then sell it under their own labels. Generally speaking, wines that have been grown, nurtured, made, and bottled under one winery's supervision are higher-quality wines.

## Appellations

"Appellation of origin" is a geographic term that indicates where the grapes are grown for a particular wine. There will be some version of this on every bottle of quality wine from almost every country. In Spain, it is Denominación de Origen, in France, it is Appellation Contrôlée (these designations also include a set of rules about how the wines are to be made). An American Viticultural Area (AVA) refers to a specific area. To include an AVA on a U.S. wine label, eighty-five percent of the grapes in the wine must come from the indicated AVA. Why should you care? Unlike milk or chocolate, wine is very much about place—that terroir word again. The climate, the soil, and other factors specific to a place figure strongly in a wine's quality and character. So it is a service to you, the consumer, to let you know exactly where a wine comes from.

## Alcohol content

Wines made around the world vary in their alcohol content, but a rough range is from seven to fifteen percent for table wines. Some, such as those from Germany and Portugal, will be in the low range of seven to nine percent, and others, as in most red and white wines from California, will be in the eleven- to fourteen-percent range. The alcohol percentage must be printed on the label and is most often on the front label of a wine bottle.

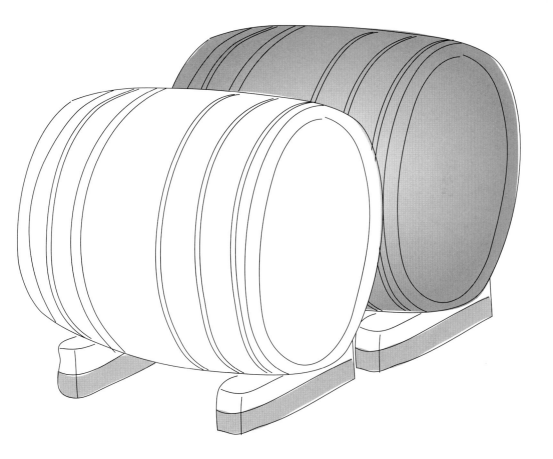

## What does "unfiltered" mean?

Unfiltered wine is wine that has not been put through a filtering process to clarify it. Wine producers may filter a wine, which means they remove small particles for greater clarity in the wine. When wine labels say "unfiltered," this means the producer has chosen not to filter the wine and wants consumers to know it. These wineries usually believe that filtering a wine during production can harm the wine and create one with less depth and character.

## Back labels

The best back labels contain the date the grapes were harvested, the varietal percentage if it is a blend of different ones, what type of oak was used, and the number of months the wine spent in oak barrels. This is often where the U.S. warning "Contains Sulfites" is located, and also where sometimes "chatty" information about a wine is written, such as the history of the winery, the type of wine, and the family who made it.

### What does "contains sulfites" mean?

Many wine labels, such as those from the United States, will say "Contains Sulfites." The use of sulfites in wine dates back over 2,000 years, but the mandatory inclusion of this information on the label by some countries is recent. Winemakers add a very small amount of sulfites, or sulfur dioxide, to wine to slow the oxidation of the wine over time. Oxidation is when the wine turns brown and the wine develops a cooked flavor and loses its fruitiness. People hypersensitive to sulfites could suffer an asthmatic attack after drinking wine or eating from a salad bar, where sulfites are often used to keep the lettuce fresh. For all but a few people, the low level of sulfites in wine presents no health hazard. If you were sensitive to sulfites, it is likely you would have known about it before you were old enough to drink wine; you could not eat from salad bars, and you could not eat shrimp and many other sea foods where sulfites are used to preserve freshness. Very few wine producers are 100 percent sulfite-free.

## Not tonight, dear; I have a headache

A friend may tell you red wines give him headaches and say he suspects it's from the sulfites contained in the wine. This is a popular belief, but it is mistaken. Many people think that sulfites cause headaches and congestion because they get headaches or congestion after drinking red wine. Actually, a typical red wine contains fewer sulfites than a typical white wine, so if you get headaches and congestion from red wines only, you are not sensitive to sulfites! What's more likely to cause headaches and congestion are the histamines that are found in the skins of grapes. Red wine will affect a histamine-sensitive wine-drinker more than white because red wine has spent more time in contact with grape skins.

Is there a special medicine for wine headaches? Well, you might try one of the dietary supplements containing vitamin B2. These are especially formulated to help prevent headaches and other discomforts by absorbing the elements in wine that can cause those discomforts. You usually take a pill with your first glass of wine, then additional pills every four to five drinks or two to three hours thereafter. The pills do not prevent intoxication and do not treat the ill effects of overindulgence in alcohol.

## A gift your host will like the most

If you're bringing wine to a dinner party, pick one that matches your host's tastes, interests and level of wine knowledge. If you know your host well, you may want to take a bottle that suits what he likes best, such as a Cabernet Sauvignon for a Cabernet-lover. If your host is planning to go to France on vacation, bring him a bottle of French wine to whet his appetite for the adventure ahead. If you're not familiar with your host or his wine preferences, select a popular wine variety such as Chardonnay or Merlot, or bring both a red and a white to cover any menu.

## When your bottle's a prize

If you have an especially valuable, rare or prized bottle you want to share with your hosts and the other guests (and taste yourself) the best thing to do is to phone ahead to inquire of your host whether your wine will go with what is being served. This way you are making an arrangement with your host to bring something specifically for dinner, you do not miss out on a prized bottle, and you do not interfere with your host's plans. Also, save special wines for small gatherings where they will receive appropriate attention.

It's so nice to be invited to a dinner party, and naturally, you want to take your host a gift of wine. The important rule to remember here is that it is a gift. Do not expect that the wine you take to a party will be served that night. To make sure your host knows you are presenting it as a gift you might even say, "This is for you to enjoy later," or "This is specially for your cellar."

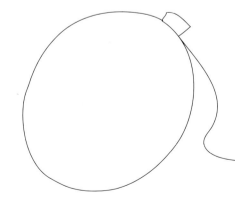

## Bottles that impress

For special occasions, such as milestone anniversaries, end-of-the-year holidays, or for a long-standing client, a hard-to-buy-for mother or a wonderful son-in-law, you'll want to select wines that match the personality of the person on your list. Ask yourself whether your recipient is likely to open the bottle soon or age it in his cellar or wine closet? If the latter, ask for a wine that ages well. Will he share it with his wife or bring it out to impress friends? If the latter, consider an impressive, large-format bottle. Does she have a favorite wine or a wine country region? If so, cater to her whims. If it's possible for you to buy direct from a winery, it's usually possible to buy a bottled signed by the winemaker or winery owner.

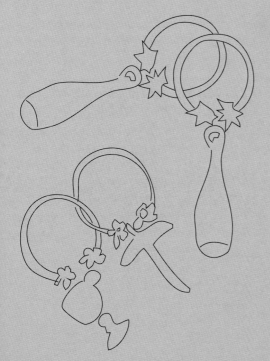

## Presenting wine

A well-chosen wine will be received with pleasure. And your gift doesn't have to come in a plain brown wrapper anymore. In fact it can be very attractively packaged since there are so many options available today. There are beautiful and unusual paper wine bags available everywhere from supermarkets to winery gift shops to fine-wine stores. If you want to think outside of the bag, however, consider unusual packages such as a planter, a canvas tote bag or an inexpensive wine bucket. You might also want to include some nice wine gadgets, such as drip stoppers, corkscrews or wine charms.

# chapter 4

# how to taste wine

Tasting wine with quiet thought, concentration, and deliberation can be a revelation. You become highly aware of how sensitive your taste buds are—and how they combine with your sense of smell to tell you about the wine that you are swishing around inside your mouth. Yes, you do need to do that—it's not some silly affectation. In fact, it's a really good way to let your taste buds (and your sense of smell) detect the finer flavors of the wine you are sampling. And what flavors you'll discover! There'll be hints of chocolate, vanilla, herbs or smoke—evoking all kinds of taste/aroma memories. Wine tasting is not reserved for the experts—anyone can learn how to do it. What's more, it's an experience that is great to share, so why not hold your own wine tasting with friends? You'll find the more you try out different wines, and the more attention you pay to each, the better you'll become at assessing a wine's quality and characteristics.

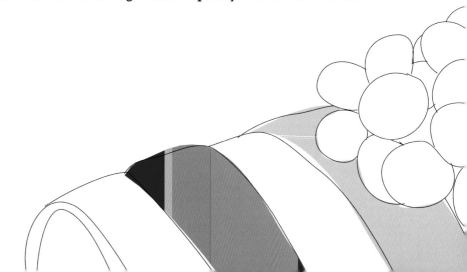

### The nose knows

Your nose, not your tongue, is the best tool for tasting wine. Why? Because your tongue recognizes only a handful of tastes, among them sweet, sour, bitter, and salty. But your sense of smell can identify thousands of substances. The reason you see wine experts make a big show of swirling their glasses, bringing the glass to their noses and inhaling is because the smell is so important in their taste perception of the wine. Most of what we think of as "taste" is actually odor. Just think about how the taste of food changes when you have a bad cold and cannot smell. So smelling the wine is not just an affectation, but the best way to tell if a wine is good or pleasing to you.

### What should wine smell like?

How do you know when a wine is good, bad or "off?" Mostly, the answer to that question depends on what kind of wine you like. But there are some quality issues that you and your nose can sniff out. The way a wine smells is dependent on many factors: the variety of the grape, the wine style, different winemaking techniques, and others. But generally a wine should smell clean, fresh, and rather like fruit. If it smells like moldy cheese, vinegar or wet cardboard, there is probably something wrong with it. (*See* page 78 for specific information on "off" smells.)

## The nose remembers, too

Aromas can help your brain remember things—like your grandmother's house, the garden in your childhood home, or your favorite leather jacket. The same is true of the wines you've drunk, since wine is something experienced primarily through your sense of smell. When you take the time to smell a wine and record its aromas in your brain, you are helping to store away a bit of knowledge about your personal wine likes and dislikes.

### wine buff

The 1976 Paris tasting was a historic moment in the wine world: A "blind" wine tasting was held in France at which French and American wines—with their identities hidden—were judged by professional French tasters. The winners in each category were wines from the Napa Valley. It was the first time in history that American wines had won out over French ones in a formal setting, and it shocked both the French and the Americans. The two winners, a Chardonnay and a Cabernet Sauvignon from two wineries in the Napa Valley, are now part of the Smithsonian Institution's "History of Wine Collection" at the Washington D.C. museum. From this point on, Napa became known as the little valley that could.

## Keep your nose clean

If you have a cold, a sinus infection or some other problem with your nose, you are not going to "taste" wine, or anything else, as well as if you were healthy. Keep that in mind before you decide you do or don't like a wine. The next time you taste it, sans your nose impairment, it will probably taste quite different. Nose drops and anything else you may put in your nose can also impair your sense of smell.

## If a wine smells bad

An instinctive feeling of revulsion is usually accurate—the wine probably is bad. Faulty corks cause wine to smell like moldy cheese or wet newspapers (see Chapter 6 for "corked" wines). A vinegar smell probably means the wine has been ruined by acetic acid. An odor of nail polish means acetate has formed in the bottle and indicates a poorly made red wine. A rotten-egg smell or a "barnyard" aroma also means things have gone wrong in the wine. Aromas of sour milk are caused by an organism called lactobacillus that spoils wine. None of these will poison you, but they all indicate inferior or spoiled wines and if these smells are present to the point that you can detect them, they will also give you bitter, sharp, dry, sour or moldy tastes.

### wine buff

Wine professionals and beginners alike use a tool called the Wine Aroma Wheel to identify wine smells. Developed at the University of California at Davis by a professor of enology, the Wine Aroma Wheel is a pie chart that gives us a common vocabulary to use in pinpointing what we smell in wine. See it on the Internet. The smallest inside circle gives general descriptions such as "fruity," "spicy" or "floral," while the larger circles grow more specific. If you determine that a wine's smell is fruity, the Wine Aroma Wheel aids in narrowing your impression to strawberry or pineapple. Why get so detailed? The more precise you can be, the more clearly you learn your own tastes—and you'll probably impress your date, too!

## Accoutrements of wine tasting

There's no need to fuss—it's not that complicated. You need the wine, of course (see chapters 1, 2, and 3 for how to choose), a few glasses suited to the type of wine you are drinking (see below), and a corkscrew you are comfortable with (see Chapter 7).

Professional tasters are usually provided with a selection of plain nibbles like crackers or bread to cleanse the palate between wines. Again, this is not just an affectation but a good idea if you want a pure taste of more than one wine and don't want one affecting the other.

## Start with a clean glass

This may seem elementary, but it is important to make sure your wine glasses are meticulously clean and not used for other things, especially milk or ice cream. These dairy products can leave residue on the inside of the glass that interferes with the delicate flavors and aromas of the wine and obscures its clarity and color. Before you pour the wine, put your nose into the empty glass and make sure you do not smell anything.

## Wine glasses

Although it's true that wine can be drunk from any kind of glass—even a paper cup or a leather bag—the right glass can enhance your experience. When buying your wine glasses, there are a few important points to keep in mind. Thin glass is better than thick. A thin, smooth rim is better than an extra ridge, or lip, of glass, which cheaper wine glasses often have. Clear glass is better than colored so you can see the wine's color. And the size and shape of the bowl, or vessel, of the glass can truly affect the wine's taste.

## What NOT to consider when choosing glasses

Aesthetics, say wine experts. The shape and design of the glass are important, but they should be designed for the particular wines you're drinking. The rules to observe are many and sometimes mysterious, but one rule is clear: Don't pick it just because it's pretty. (See Chapter 7 for more information on wine glasses.)

## How to hold your wine glass

The reason most wine glasses have a stem is because you are supposed to hold them by the stem and not smudge the glass bowl with your fingertips. This allows you to better see the color and clarity of the wine and is more appetizing for most people! A room full of wine snobs would be aghast to see someone gumming up the glass with the same fingers that just dipped a chip, but most people probably wouldn't notice. When your hands touch the bowl of the glass, body heat will warm the wine a bit, so if your wine is too cold, there may be a point to holding it the "wrong" way.

## Playing the flute

Champagne flutes are so elegant and stylish. Remember that it is important—and part of the fun—to be able to see the path of bubbles traveling up the long narrow glass. That's why you should always hold your flute by its stem. Champagne is always at its best best when served quite cold, so you also want to avoid warming the flute with your hands.

---

### wine buff

The old-fashioned shape of a Champagne glass known as a *coupe*—round, broad, and shallow—is said to have been specially modeled after the breasts of Marie Antoinette, the notorious former queen of France. These saucer-like glasses provided very little room for the tiny bubbles of sparkling wine to travel up the glass before they burst. Like Marie herself, the once ubiquitous, old-fashioned shape was guillotined in favor of the tall, narrow flute designed to make the most of the bubbles.

---

## How to swirl, girl

Professional wine tasters have oodles of confidence. They can effortlessly swirl wine in the glass without spilling a drop. Don't try that without plenty of practice. The safest way is to place your glass on a secure table in front of you and hold it by its stem at the lower end between your thumb and index finger or your first two fingers, whichever feels more comfortable. Rotate the glass in a circular motion fast enough so that the wine swirls around in the glass, but not so fast that it spills over. This is why professionals and wine knowledgeable people never fill a glass to the brim.

### Why you swirl

You swirl the wine in your glass to get the most out of your wine's aroma. The motion releases the aromas of the wine so that you are better able to appreciate them. The smell of a wine, when it is clean and lacking any "off" odors, should be an enticing prelude to what you are about to taste, so don't deny yourself the experience! In a young wine, you should detect fruit and maybe the smell of the barrels it was aged in. If the wine is older, you'll notice less fruit and more complexity.

### Sniff, sniff

After you've swirled your wine a few times, put your nose into the center of the glass. The aromas are enclosed in the glass so your nose should not be too distant from it. Inhale a few times. If you do not get any smell, swirl again, then sniff again. Some wines need to sit in the glass for a while before they "open up" and offer their full-on aromas.

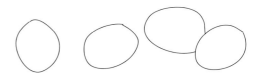

### wine buff

Red wine can stain and darken your teeth. Wine-drinkers always want to know how to clean red wine stains on clothes, tablecloths or carpets (*see* Chapter 7 for a few tips), but few realize that if you drink a fair amount of it, red wine can stain or darken your teeth just as coffee and tea do. How do you remove red-wine stains from teeth or prevent them from happening if you drink a lot of red wine? There is nothing you can do to the wine (except switch to drinking white) that would prevent staining. Your best bet to remove stains is to prevent them from happening by brushing your teeth as soon as you can after consuming red wine. For bad staining, consult a dentist.

### Red-wine color

When you are first served a wine, hold the glass at an angle so the wine is almost sideways in the glass against a light or white background in a well-lit room. Look for clarity and a deep purple or brick red in a red wine. The color comes from the contact of grape juice with grape skins during the winemaking process and, in the making of red wines, this can be an extended period. Older red wines grow less intense in color as they age. Red wines will lose some of their cherry redness or purplish hue and take on a brownish tone. If you see a brownish tint around the edge of the wine in your glass in a young red wine, beware, as it has probably oxidized prematurely and is not going to be pleasant to drink.

## White-wine color

Look for clarity and a pale-straw, light-green or gold color in a white wine. White wines are pale because their juice is pressed immediately and does not come into extended contact with grape skins during the winemaking process. All older white wines deepen in color and grow more golden in color with age. If a young white has a brownish tinge, there is probably something wrong with it and you will not enjoy its taste.

Don't be color-blind! Use another of your senses—your sight—and take a good look at your wine before you quaff it. The real pro will hold the glass against a clean white background for perfect viewing. A winemaker will give a lot of attention to a wine's color and it is usually an eye-pleasing aspect of the drink. Whether it is the deep, ruby color of a Cabernet Sauvignon, the pale-salmon color of a rosé, or the honeyed amber of a dessert wine, wine can look arresting as well as appetizing on the dinner table, buffet table or in your glass.

## Wine sludge

If you notice solids collected at the bottom of your glass or bottle of wine, especially in an older wine, this is not a sign that something has gone wrong with the wine. Older wines will sometimes have what wine pros call "sediment" in the bottle. It is not bad for you and won't affect the taste of the wine, but many people find it unappealing to look at or to feel on their tongues. Decanting, or pouring the wine into another container and leaving the sediment behind in the bottle, will usually do the trick. (See Chapter 7 for details on decanting.) If you are not entertaining, you may simply want to pour from the bottle through a small, fine-meshed strainer directly into your glass.

## Hold your tongue

To effectively taste the wine, you should make sure you do not have a riot of flavors coating your mouth and fighting your taste buds before you try it. Let's say you have never tried a wine before and want to see if you will like the grape variety or the style of a certain wine producer. Make sure your first few sips (and take a few, since your mouth must adapt to the wine) are not clouded by a horseradish-encrusted halibut or a pizza liberally sprinkled with hot red pepper. After you've really tasted the wine, then feel free to go ahead and try drinking it with your hot peppers or horseradish! After all, food and wine are natural partners.

## Baby, it's really cold inside...your glass

Another thing that factors into your ability to taste the wine is its temperature. Common mistakes are to serve and drink wine at too cold a temperature for whites and rosés, and too warm a temperature for reds. All wines, even reds, should be served slightly cooler than at modern room temperature. As with cheese, when the wine is too cold, many of the more subtle flavors and aromas are killed off. When the wine is too warm, its alcohol can jump out at you.

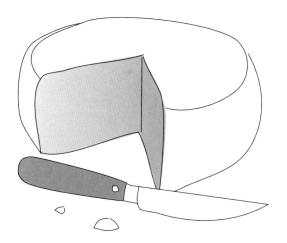

## Tasting with your tongue

Different parts of the tongue register different tastes, so when you take a sip of wine, hold it in your mouth and let the wine roll over your tongue. Wine experts and professional tasters sometimes swish it around in their mouths like mouthwash, but you may only wish to do this when you are alone! As you hold the wine in your mouth, notice its texture. Notice if there is some tartness to the wine (its acidity). Take note of the astringency in a red wine (its tannins)—hopefully it will not be so mouth-puckering that your tongue rebels. Notice if there is a pleasant fruit flavor, maybe several layers of flavors, and a pleasurable aftertaste. These are the hallmarks of a well-made wine.

## A few helpful hints

### Order to drink in

If you are tasting several wines in a short period—at a multi-course dinner, perhaps, or a wine-tasting party (*see* Chapter 8 for how to organize a home wine tasting)—it is wise to drink them in a certain order so your palate is not overwhelmed early on. In general, white wines should be drunk before reds, dry wines should be drunk before sweet ones, and young wines should be drunk before older ones.

### Mood counts, too

Once you consider the size and type of wine glass, the temperature of the wine, the order they are drunk in, and all the other minutiae of formal wine tasting, remember, too, that if you are hot, tired, cranky, hungry, full, recovering from a cold or just coming down with one, then all these factors can affect what you get from a wine you are drinking. What tastes bad or mediocre to you one day may light up your taste buds the next time you drink it under more favorable circumstances. Or it can work the other way around. Consider these circumstances the next time you want to write off a wine as not being one you like.

### Write it down

Most professional tasters keep copious notes of their tasting experiences. You do not have to, of course, but you may find it helpful to briefly record some of the impressions of wines you taste, particularly ones you like and want to remember next time you order wine. What does it look like, smell like, and taste like? What does it remind you of? Why do you like it: because it's soft or crisp, rich or light, fruity or powerfully tannic? Taking the time to consider these questions and making the extra effort to write them down—however briefly—will help you.

Don't drink alone—wine is even better when shared. If you have friends who are interested in wine—whether experienced or novices—taste wines together with them, perhaps at a wine-tasting party you host. When you taste with others, especially those with more experience than you, you can share your impressions and experiences of the wines and learn from them.

## Side by side

One of the most helpful tricks in wine tasting, and something professional tasters do all the time, is to taste different wines together. This aids the taster in making comparisons when judging the quality of wines, but to a novice it is especially helpful because it also aids in learning what you like. Don't know the difference between a Cabernet Sauvignon and a Pinot Noir? Try both side by side and note the very real differences in taste, aroma, and body. Think all white wines taste alike? Taste a German Riesling next to a California Chardonnay and never again will you hold that opinion.

how to taste wine

## Describing what you taste

There is a scientific basis for many of the words used to describe wine. How can a wine smell like grapefruit or taste like eucalyptus? Because wine grapes share many of the naturally occurring chemical compounds found in fruits, flowers, and herbs. There is a body of wine taste descriptors that have been developed (see Chapter 6 for a glossary of wine terms) but, really, anything goes. Any words you can think of that best depict the taste and aroma sensations you get from a wine are helpful in understanding what you like and what you want to order or buy next time. So don't shy away from being creative!

## Flavors and aromas in white wines

Let yourself explore. The fruit flavors and aromas most often detected in white wines include various citrus fruits such as oranges, grapefruit, lemons, and limes; other fruits like lychees, peaches, and apricots; various tropical fruits like pineapple and mango; plus gooseberries, apples, figs, and melon. Other flavors that are often detected in white wines include vanilla, butter or butterscotch, rose petals, nut flavors, and toast.

## What you may taste in popular whites

In Chardonnay, many people detect apple, banana, and pear aromas and flavors, as well as butter, vanilla, and oak. In Sauvignon Blanc, tasters often detect aromas reminiscent of bell pepper, grass, asparagus, gooseberries, and green beans, along with flavors of grapefruit, other citrus fruits, pineapple, and flowers. In Gewürztraminer, you might note spices such as cinnamon, clove or allspice, plus flowery notes, grapefruit, peach, apricot, and lychee flavours. In Rieslings, you could find jasmine, roses, orange blossom, citrus fruit, lemon peel, peach, apricot, pineapple, melon, apple, and honey.

Do all Chardonnays (or Rieslings or Merlots) taste alike? Well, no. Don't be surprised if many a Chardonnay has tickled your taste buds and then you come upon one that makes you gag. It may be that there is nothing wrong with the wine at all—except that you don't like it. This can have everything to do with the style of the wine producer. Some winemakers strive for a lean, crisp Chardonnay while others make it rich and creamy. Many wine professionals say wine is like art, and while that may be overstating the case, winemakers are creative people who influence greatly the outcome of their own wine. So while everyone may be making a Chardonnay while the market demands it, there will be a great range of styles to choose from.

## Flavors and aromas in red wines

The flavors and aromas most commonly detected in red wines include various berries, such as cherry, black cherry, raspberry, strawberry, blackberry, and raisins and vegetal flavors such as green pepper. Other flavors detected in red wines include jam (cooked red or black fruit), black pepper, chocolate, spice, herbs, mint, currant, plum, eucalyptus, anise, tobacco, smoke, leather, and "farmyard" tones.

## What you may taste in popular reds

The answer is, a huge range. In Pinot Noir, mint, anise, vanilla, coffee, soy, and leather are often detected. In Merlot, you might find blackcurrant, blackberry, black cherry, vegetable, herb, and oak flavors. In a Cabernet Sauvignon, tasters often note flavors of raspberry, cassis, green pepper, olives, eucalyptus, mint, black pepper, vanilla, chocolate, coffee, oak, and soy. And in Zinfandel, you could taste smoke, raspberry, and chocolate.

### wine buff

There are coopers who specialize in making oak barrels solely for storing and aging wine. High-quality grapes may be the key component to making fine wine, but prime oak barrels are another critical ingredient. For specific wines, some winemakers source barrels in the forests of France to make sure they are getting the best wood that is seasoned, cured, and aged in the right way, then shaped into barrels and "toasted" by highly skilled coopers. Oak barrels have been around for 4,000 years and winemakers consider them a significant component in winemaking since they soften wine and enrich its flavors and aromas. A wine's texture and spice flavors also derive from barrel-aging.

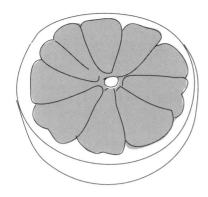

## What flavors you may taste in dessert wines

The lush, sweet flavors and aromas commonly found in dessert wines include honey, honeysuckle, apricot nectar, orange peel, figs, butterscotch, caramel, ripe, juicy peaches, citrus fruits, and gardenias.

## Tasting rosés

Dry rosés, especially those from California and Europe, commonly have red-fruit flavors and aromas such as raspberry, strawberry, and cherry. But since these rosés can be made from grapes as varied as Cabernet Franc, Zinfandel and Pinot Noir, the flavors and aromas vary widely, too. So-called blush wines, created in California, are sweet, soft, and fruity and commonly contain flavors and aromas of strawberries, watermelon, ripe pear, honeysuckle, and sweet citrus fruit.

## The aromas and flavors in sparkling wines

Sparkling wines and Champagnes can be made in a variety of ways, from bone-dry and crisp to round and creamy. Flavors and aromas commonly found in sparkling wines include hazelnut, brioche or biscuit, meringue, lemons, apples, figs, pears, citrus fruit, white peaches and nectarines, almonds, licorice, vanilla, caramel, red and black cherries, currants, and strawberries.

### What is a "blind tasting?"

No, you don't have to wear a blindfold. A blind wine tasting is one in which you taste several wines without knowing what they are. The wines may be decanted in plain glass containers, or the bottles may be hidden in brown paper bags. The idea is to go one-on-one with the wine, free of any preconceived notions about what winery or wine region of the world the wine is from, how much it costs, and even what grape it is made from. Professional tasters often taste "blind," and it may be fun for you to try it with your friends. (See Chapter 8 for details of how to set up a wine tasting at home.)

### Why treasure older red wines?

Tannins, the astringent and bitter chemical compounds found in grape seeds and skins, help give red wines their aging potential. (They are found in white wines, too, but in much less concentration.) They give off both a flavor and a tactile feeling in your mouth and help preserve the wine over time.

Tannins change over that time, too, progressing from young and hard to mellow and soft. So you can actually watch (or taste) your red wine's gradual development over many years. A special delight for wine collectors is to taste a bottle each year from a specially chosen case of a red wine to note how it evolves over time.

### Wine camp

As wine consumption grows and new wine regions emerge from around the world, so, too, have wine entertainment and education opportunities. You can further your tasting experiences and deepen your wine knowledge by attending a weekend at a wine "boot camp," a week-long food-and-wine vacation, or simply by dropping into a local wine festival over the weekend. Or give these opportunities as gifts to a wine-loving spouse or parent. Search the Internet or contact wineries, wine societies, cooking schools, or food societies in your area.

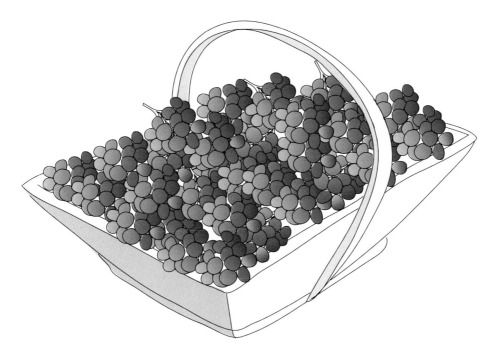

## Hands-on learning

If you are looking for something more sustained and in-depth to boost your wine knowledge, and want to participate in a dynamic experience with others similarly inclined, look at local colleges for a wine class or food-and-wine classes. If you are lucky enough to live in or near a wine-producing region, the resources will be limitless. If you live in an urban area, wine professionals—whether writers, sommeliers or wine company executives—may live there or be visiting and may teach courses or give presentations on wine. A little research will probably yield a bounty of opportunities.

### wine buff

Winemakers are divided on what is the most important aspect of producing wine. Some say the most critical element is how they farm the grapes in the vineyards, while others believe it's the winemaker's skill at manipulating the grapes after they are picked. In the first group, winemakers say nature itself does the real creative job and it's their duty to merely shepherd the grapes along to the wines they were meant to be. Many of these winemakers also practice organic or "sustainable" farming methods in order to be as gentle as possible with their wine grapes.

# chapter 5

# how to store wine at home

As you begin to appreciate wine more deeply, you'll find that you'll want to start collecting a few bottles to keep at home. This makes good sense for several reasons. For instance, you may have found an excellent wine that is on sale at a bargain price when you buy a case or two. So, if you're not going to drink it immediately, how do you keep it in perfect condition? And how do you choose which wines to keep in order to improve their overall quality and flavor? How long should they be stored? And at what temperature? Is there some mysterious secret to maintaining a wine cellar? Relax! Keeping wine at home, whether it's in a simple storage rack or a fully equipped cellar is no longer the preserve of royalty. Anyone can have a small store of wine at home. Its just a matter of deciding how much you want to keep and what available space you have to store it in.

## Why store wine?

Okay, let's get real. The average bottle of wine is probably aged about half an hour—between the time you bought it at the store and you hand it over to the host of the dinner party. And most wines, especially inexpensive and table wines, are meant to be drunk within a year or two. But that said, one of the enjoyable things about some wines is that they keep. Beer and sake (Japanese rice wine) are best when drunk fresh, not aged, and this is true for some white wines, too. But other whites, such as Alsace Riesling, white burgundy, and Loire Chenin Blanc, can age five years or longer and many reds keep for as long as ten or more. They not only keep, they evolve and improve over time. This is what experts mean when they refer to "aging" a wine.

How do you decide whether to enjoy your wine now or save it for later? Well, just think of wine like a handsome youth. Will he grow into a distinguished man, still handsome but with the added quality of maturity and wisdom? Or will he merely add a beer belly and lose his hair? Generally speaking, most white wines, rosés, blush wines, and Champagnes should be enjoyed when they are young—within a couple of years of their vintage dates or from the time you bought them, in the case of non-vintage Champagne. Most red wines, however, like the handsome youth who grows even more desirable with age, will benefit from some aging.

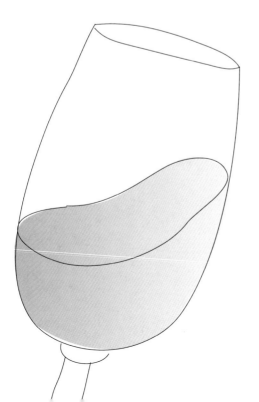

## Where to keep it

Whether or not you plan to age it, keep your wine—from one bottle to 1,000—in a dark, cool, vibration-free environment such as a humid basement, a special wine refrigerator, or a closet. Although many a design magazine will feature glamorous kitchen makeovers with built-in wine storage among the kitchen cabinets, a kitchen is often the worst place to store wine, due to its fluctuation in temperatures and its smells.

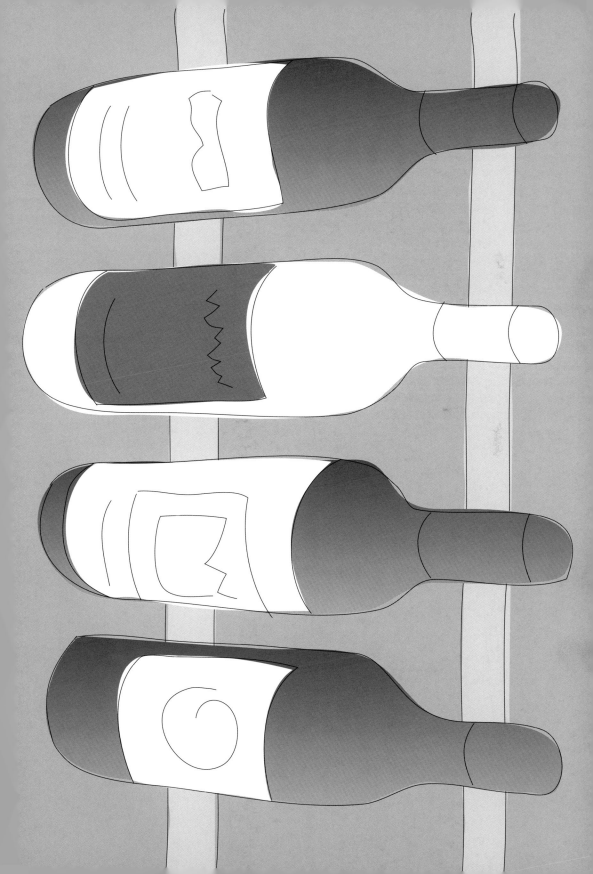

## You don't need to get fancy

Wine storage systems—whether they are in the form of cabinets, wine racks or special wine refrigerators—have become stylish status symbols. Nowadays there is a multitude of choices available, ranging from two-bottle stainless-steel racks to 1,000-bottle mahogany cabinets. But this is sometimes more a question of style than substance. Russian émigré André Tchelistcheff, a chemist-turned-winemaker who influenced the development of the Napa Valley wine industry in the mid-1900s, stored his wine under his bed!

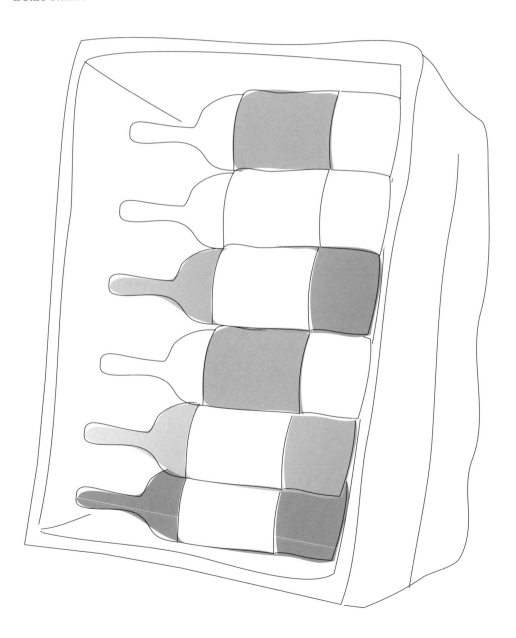

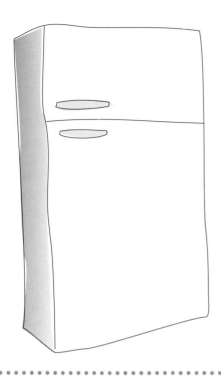

## Store it in the refrigerator?

The temperature of the average home refrigerator is around 40°F (4°C). You shouldn't drink wines that cold (wines show best at higher temperatures) and it is also too cold for optimum wine storage for the long-term. Most professional cellars employ temperatures from 55° to 65°F/12° to.18°C. It is a mistake to store a half-dozen bottles of wine in your refrigerator to drink over many months because you run the risk of harming the wine in the bottles. The refrigerator's constant vibrations can hurt it, and its low humidity level may cause the cork to loosen and the wine to oxidize. (See Chapter 6 for more details about oxidation.)

## Sideshow

Why do you always see wine bottles lying on their sides? Because keeping the liquid in the bottle in contact with the cork keeps the cork moist and plump and the bottle sealed. If the cork dries out and allows air into the bottle, the wine is spoiled. For wine you will age for thirty minutes, this is not an issue, but if you have even a few bottles and are not sure when you will drink them, lay them on their sides to ensure that they are safe.

### wine buff

Natural caves dug into mountainsides have provided ideal shelter for wines for thousands of years. The long tunnels of darkness hold not only wine barrels but also cobwebs, bats, gouges left by the laborers who dug them, old bottles, and even older memories. Some of the early wines caves in California date back to the 1800s, and many in Europe are much older than that. Vintners in times past found that the underground chambers were ideal for housing wine in barrels because of their cool temperatures and high humidity levels—optimal for aging wines. Today state-of-the-art wineries can still see the advantage of wine caves and their interest for visitors, so new ones are being created every day.

## Temperatures

The best conditions for storing wine include stable temperatures around 55° to 65°F/12° to18°C, humidity of approximately eighty percent and darkness, which is basically the environment of a cave. Cool temperatures slow the aging process, allowing for better development of the wine over time. Temperature fluctuations cause wine to expand and contract, which can push the cork out and expose the wine to oxygen. This spoils the wine, turning it brownish and giving it a cooked or baked flavor like sherry (see "oxidation" in the Chapter 6 glossary). Very dry storage conditions may also cause exposure to oxygen.

## When darkness falls

Wine stored in darkness retains its clarity. Light reacts to proteins in the wine to form a haze as well as other undesirable effects such as "off" aromas and flavors. Basements and closets (even the spaces under beds) are best for these reasons, and professionally built wine cellars, rooms, and cabinets are all designed to leave your bottles in the dark.

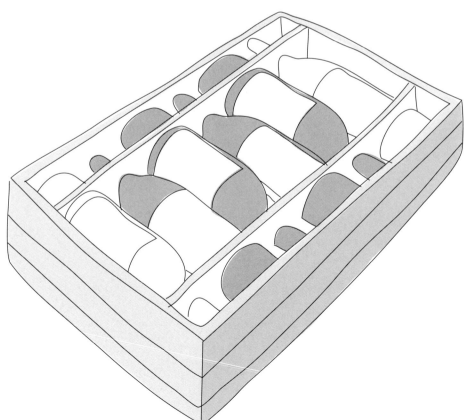

## Collecting may save you money

Starting a wine collection may sound like a costly proposition and you may turn off to the idea right away, especially if you are a novice or only an occasional drinker. But consider this: Collecting, or having an inventory of wines at home, may actually save you money. It'll certainly save you time when you've been invited to a last-minute dinner or you forgot to buy a bottle for your mother's birthday dinner. You can save money by purchasing by the case—sometimes even purchasing a half-case will earn you a discount—and taking advantage of sales by stocking up on several bottles. When you buy each bottle you need or want at the last moment from what's available at non-sale prices, you lose both time and money.

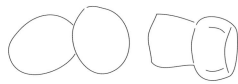

## Rent or buy?

If there is no suitable place to store wine in your home and you would like to stock up on wine or collect it even on a small scale, you can buy wine storage systems, such as cabinets or refrigerators with insulation and adjustable temperature and humidity controls, or rent lockers or other spaces in warehouses dedicated to storing wine. These should be climate- and humidity-controlled spaces. They are most prevalent in wine-production regions, but are increasingly available in urban areas, too. Some people with a big wine-collecting habit even use them to hide wine from their spouses!

## Going all the way

If you get bitten by the wine-collecting bug, you may want to invest in a fully outfitted wine cellar. These can include such equipment as wine racks, refrigeration units, humidifiers, and other accoutrements, and can cost anywhere from a few hundred dollars for a mini-unit wine refrigerator to hundreds of thousands of dollars for a custom-built wine cellar that is an additional room in your home. The bigger and more valuable your wine collection, the more you will want to invest in proper wine storage to protect it. Generally, there are three key elements to effective wine storage at this level: adequate insulation, airtight construction, and an appropriate cooling system.

### wine buff

From the beginning of civilization, art and wine have been closely interconnected. According to legend, Pegasus, the winged horse of Greek mythology, gave birth to wine and the arts when his hooves unleashed the sacred Spring of the Muses. The spring waters tapped the roots of the vines and thus inspired the artists and poets who drank the fruit of the vine. Wineries and museums around the world display images of how wine and winemaking have been depicted in art through the ages to show how wine has been an inspirational muse for thousands of years.

### Wine rooms

Prefabricated wine rooms are usually designed to require assembly at home. There are several manufacturers of walk-in wine rooms, and their products differ only slightly. The types that come with wooden racks for wine bottles are probably preferable to a combination of aluminum and wood wine racks, since they cut down on vibrations. Bottle capacities in wine rooms can range from 700 to 2,500-plus. These wine storage systems are probably the most cost-effective per bottle of the many choices available.

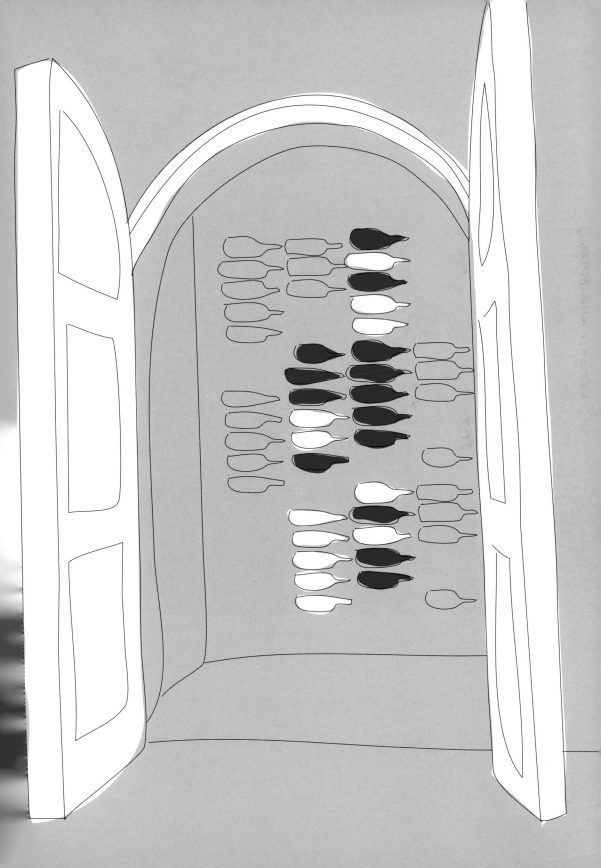

## Wine cabinets

Another wine-storage option is a refrigerated cabinet, made of wood or stainless steel, that is attractive enough to incorporate into your living spaces and doesn't have to be hidden in a closet or basement. They can be freestanding or built in. There are many manufacturers throughout the world that make units that can hold anywhere from fifty to 2,500 bottles. Mini-units with capacities of twenty-four to 100 bottles can fit beneath your kitchen cabinets or in a wet bar in a living or family room. These claim to protect small wine collections just as well as any larger, more expensive system.

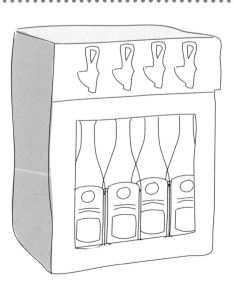

## Wine dispensers

Among the many gadgets people with a wine collection or some wine inventory at home may find useful is a wine dispenser system. They will maintain your opened wines for up to three weeks, retarding oxidation, which means they eliminate the risk of spoilage. These systems give you "wine storage in a bottle." Used both in homes and at restaurants and bars, the systems preserve the wine with nitrogen and can work for a single bottle or a few cases of wine.

## Wine blending kit

If you want to get more involved with wine, you can even try your hand at making your own blend of wine at home—alone or with a few friends. Merchants are selling wine-blending and -tasting kits, which contain everything needed to whip up your own unique red-wine blend as the pros do in Bordeaux. The kits typically include an instruction booklet, glass pipettes, drip stops, blending note sheets, and blind tasting bottle covers. You can learn the methods used in the Bordeaux tradition of French winemaking—or just enjoy drinking your concoction.

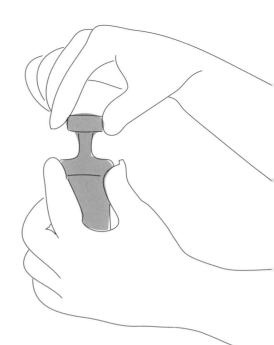

### wine buff

The world's largest museum of wine, food and the arts is located in Napa, California. Copia: The American Center for Wine, Food and the Arts, which opened in 2001, is a cultural museum and educational center dedicated to exploring the American contribution to the worlds of wine and food in close association with the arts and humanities. Cooking and wine-tasting classes, and tours of its fertile, organic gardens are conducted daily. Its outdoor concert terrace features musical performances, and there are art exhibits that illustrate and celebrate the role of wine and food in American culture. "Copia" is the Greek goddess of abundance.

### What kind of wines should I store?

It makes sense to store mostly reds because more red wines than white wines improve with age. Tannins, the astringent, bitter group of compounds found in the seeds and skins of grapes, help add to red wine's aging potential (as does acidity) by slowing oxidation. A young wine has new, bitter tannins but after a wine is bottled, the tannins help preserve it and help it develop increasingly complex flavors and aromas over time.

### Which wines are best to store?

Many Cabernet Sauvignon wines and Bordeaux blends (which usually use Cabernet Sauvignon in their blends) will continue to improve for ten to fifteen years after the vintage date with proper storage. Pinot Noir and Zinfandel wines can also improve with age—possibly as much as five to ten years after their vintage dates. If you have more than one bottle of the same wine, you might try aging one for a few years and tasting it and then trying the same wine a couple of years later. Even if it's hard for you to remember what the earlier one tasted like—and this is where keeping notes will help—at least you'll be certain of having have two pleasurable drinking experiences!

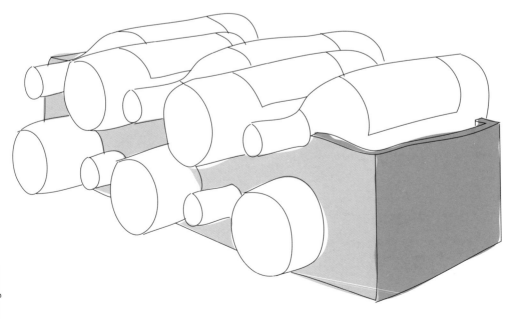

### wine buff

The oldest evidence for the existence of wine comes from at least 5000 B.C., according to the U.S. scientific journal *Nature*. The earliest-known wine-drinkers appear to have been Neolithic villagers not far from Lake Urmia, in what is now northeastern Iran. Evidence of wine, resembling Greek retsina (a wine flavored with pine resin, still popular today in Greece), was found in jars placed along the kitchen walls of a mud-brick structure. Researchers believe that wine was traditionally used to accompany food because of the jars' location near the kitchen. They also believe wine may have had religious connotations, because in later periods fermentation was depicted as a "magical" process due to its bubbles and its end product's resulting effect on the body and mind.

how to store wine at home

## Vintage charts

Vintage charts, which rate years and advise you on what was "a good year" and what wasn't, can be useful guides for deciding what's worth collecting and aging. The most useful charts are broken down by grape variety, country or wine region, and note both the vintage quality and the aging potential of the wine. Vintage charts can be a handy reference for the novice and connoisseur alike, but they are somewhat broad in scope and thus should not be taken as gospel.

## Ask a friend

Collecting wine isn't simply a matter of going out to amass whatever you can lay your hands on and have the cash to buy. There are questions of what to buy, how much to buy, where to get it, what to pay for it, how to store it, how to organize it, and when to drink it. Unless you don't mind making some costly mistakes at first, you should take a class on the topic from the local wine and food society, check out a book from the library, or seek out a friend or acquaintance who has a wine collection and ask him or her for do's and don'ts. Don't be too impulsive—it's always helpful to learn from others' mistakes, successes, and research.

## Is collecting a "guy thing"?

Now that's an interesting question. Many more men collect wine than women, although more women are starting to collect wines and build wine cellars. Women generally have more sensitive and finely tuned palates than men and many are passionate about good wine, but they are not collectors because they expect to drink the wines they buy—not resell them for investment or keep them as prized possessions. Retailers say that even when women buy a wine to keep for some time, they usually also plan to serve it at a special occasion.

## Do you think like a collector?

Many wine collectors think of the wines they collect as things they have to own. They may not even intend to consume them; they simply love looking at the bottles or they love the idea that the bottles are part of their cellar. Just thinking about their collections is a pleasurable experience for true die-hard collectors. There can also be an element of competition in the collector mentality: a my-collection-is-bigger-and-better-than-yours attitude.

The problem of knowing how to collect wine deters many people from even starting. So let's make it a little easier for you. Are there particular varieties, say Chardonnay and Merlot, or wine regions of the world that you favor? If so, start a collection with those and move on from there. As you taste and experience wines more fully, you may come up with new categories of your own that you will want to add to your collection. For instance, you could explore New Zealand Sauvignon Blancs, Pinot Noir from around the world, or dry rosés from Mediterranean countries.

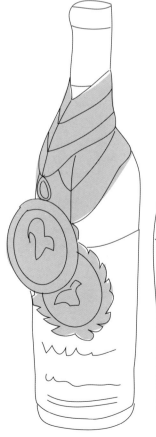

## What to stock

You needn't have a large or expensive group of wines to call yourself a collector. It's the thought and enthusiasm that count. So while "serious" collectors may invest in extensive ranges of French wines from Bordeaux and Burgundy, California's cult Cabernet Sauvignons, and Italian Super Tuscans, you might just want a handy stock of affordable wines to drink when friends drop by or for when there is an unexpected victory, anniversary, or milestone to celebrate.

## Seeking help

As when ordering wine in a restaurant or buying it in a store, seek out a good wine merchant for advice on what to stock up on for your home wine inventory. Make sure you can explain your tastes and how often you drink—or would like to drink—reds, whites, rosés, and/or Champagnes, and ask for help in forming a buying plan. Depending on your budget, this might only mean a few bottles a month, but it will help you organize your thoughts and your wine collection.

## How much to buy

Even if budget isn't a great consideration, you should still think about limiting the amount of wine you buy to the amount you can actually drink, entertain with or give as gifts before the wine runs out of steam. In other words, certain types of wine don't last forever and you do not want to get over-excited about a white wine or a rosé, buy five cases of it, drink one, and then forget about it for three years. That could be a big mistake, as your remaining four cases may not be drinkable. On the other hand, if you had bought five cases of Cabernet Sauvignon and stored it properly, you'd be safe. So keep aging time and your drinking pattern in mind when thinking about how much to buy.

## Do you have a taste for older wines?

Another thing to consider when deciding what to buy and collect is whether you like aged wines. In addition to experiencing a softening of the astringent tannins of their youth, red wines lose their bold fruitiness with age. Before you invest in a case or two of expensive French or California red wine to age for ten years or longer, experiment with older wines by buying a few bottles at a retail store or restaurant and tasting them to see if they suit your fancy. If you don't like the taste, it probably won't much matter to you how they have "evolved" over time.

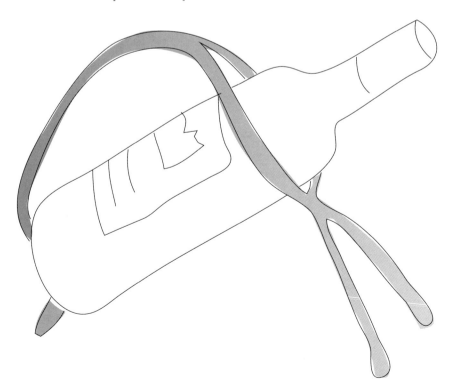

Healthful and nutritious aspects of wine have been recognized by doctors for thousands of years. Around 450 B.C., the Greek father of medicine, Hippocrates, recommended specific wines as diuretics, to purge fever, disinfect and dress wounds, and as nutritional supplements. The oldest known wine book was written by a French doctor around A.D. 1410. Because the acids and alcohol in wine kill germs and harmful microbes, it was considered a safer drink than water up until the eighteenth century.

how to store wine at home

## What accoutrements do I need for a collection?

None, really. If you follow the rules above for keeping your wine safe—a dark, cool, stable place—then you really don't need much else. Of course, people love to get into a subject once they discover its joys, and often this means acquiring gadgets and paraphernalia. Wine is no exception—the paraphernalia exists and the zeal of collectors exists. But before you start buying grape vintage wall clocks, California wine maps, digital hygrometers, and custom-built redwood shelves, remember that you can also store your wine in the cardboard boxes it came in—as long as you tip the boxes gently on their sides.

## Organizing it

One of the most important things you'll find most helpful in the long run is to organize your collection properly. Even if you only have a couple of cases, unless the bottles are all the same, you should have a rational plan for organizing it. Put the wines you'd likely drink sooner rather than later within arm's reach. Stash wines worth aging or ones you view as seasonal—such as summer rosés—behind or below them. If your inventory is growing, consider an inventory sheet where you can list the type of wine, the vintage, the year purchased, the price, and when you want to or should drink it. Computer software for this is available if you want to get high-tech about it, or when your collection is growing rapidly.

## Practical considerations

Make sure the place you are storing wines can be illuminated when you need to go through it and find something. The wine should rest in the dark, but you should not have to be in the dark about where it is, nor grope your way around in a dark basement looking for a particular bottle. Your wine-storage space should also be easily accessible and spacious enough so that you can move around in it.

# chapter **6**

# what "wine talk" really means

Don't worry if you sometimes feel totally confused by some of the terms commonly used by writers to describe a wine's unique qualities. Some commentators may seem to be speaking a completely different language from yours. And it's certainly true that experts can fall into the trap of becoming far too esoteric when discussing wine. As a result, it's easy to be intimidated by all the jargon that's being thrown around. You just feel that others are playing a game of one-upmanship with fanciful concepts. So, what do all these terms such as "noses" and "length" really mean? Does full-bodied mean that the wine is good? And what kind of person would drink something that smells like a sweaty saddle or cat pee? Relax! It's not so difficult when you allow your own imagination to explore freely—and, if you don't agree with someone else's descriptive terms, that's fine. Trust your own experience and your own palate.

## Say what?

"Winespeak," the words wine writers and other wine professionals use to talk about wine, is a language all its own. Many people scoff at the sometimes esoteric or silly-sounding lingo wine experts often use to describe wines, but the professionals themselves defend their use of such language by saying that someone had to develop a language or set of terms to analyze and describe the taste sensations, feelings, and experiences that wine evokes in people. Both sides have a point—it's all just a matter of perspective.

I don't go overboard on "winespeak" when talking about wine. But it's often really useful to borrow from the language used to describe food—so I might use words such as "spice," "chocolate," "apple," "cherry," "vanilla," "honey," and "coffee." This is because wine consists of more than 200 chemical compounds, many of which are identical or similar to those found in fruits, vegetables, spices, herbs, and other substances. Both wine and food leave flavors on the palate, and the same molecules that give bananas or chocolate their tastes can show up in a wine. Many wine flavors and aromas mimic those of food.

## Pass me that sexy, voluptuous wine immediately!

Wine writers often use words to describe wines that involve things we never put in our mouths (and would never want to) such as "sweaty saddle leather," "earth," "tobacco," and even "cat pee" (often detected in Sauvignon Blanc). These flavors and aromas come from chemical compounds in the wine. They can be one drinker's turn-off and another's cup of tea (or goblet of wine). In an expanding effort to explain themselves, wine writers and other wine professionals are also bestowing personality and physical traits upon wine such as "elegant," "brooding," "voluptuous," "snappy," "sassy," and "sexy." If these terms make sense to you and fit your experience of drinking a wine, use them to think of wines in ways that distinguish one from another. That way, you can best determine and remember the wines you enjoy the next time that wine list comes around. If they don't make sense to you, forget them. You don't have to use someone else's vocabulary to enjoy the wine!

## A useful wine glossary

Following is a practical glossary of wine terms, wine descriptors and "technical" terms that wine producers, vendors, and writers often use.

### Acidity

A wine's natural acids give it a crisp or tart taste. Natural acids in the wine grapes produce this crispness. Grapes, and thus wine, have three primary acids: tartaric, malic, and citric. A wine may often be described as "high (or low) in acidity".

### Aroma

Odor has more to do with taste than your tongue does; your nose can identify more than 2,000 different odors while your tongue tastes four main tastes: sweet, salty, bitter, and sour. There is also a fifth taste the Japanese have discovered called umami which translates best as "savory". A wine's aroma is the smell of the wine; common descriptors for wine's aromas include "fruity," "floral," and "earthy." Technically, the aroma differs from its "bouquet" (see page 122).

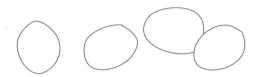

### Astringent

This is a tactile sensation, best described as the mouth-puckering feeling you get when drinking certain red wines. This drying sensation in the mouth comes from strong or young tannins.

### Balance

This refers to the relationship between the major components in a wine: acidity, fruit, alcohol, and tannin. None of these components should exist out of balance from the others. Another way of saying this is that all these major components are in harmony with each other. Balance alters over time. If a wine writer says a wine is "out of balance", it is a fundamental flaw.

## Barrel-fermented

White wine fermented in an oak barrel instead of a stainless-steel tank. Chardonnays are often made this way, as are some Sauvignon Blanc. Stainless steel gives leaner, more austere flavors compared to the fuller flavors produced by oak fermentation.

## Blanc de blancs (literally "white of whites")

Any wine made solely from white grapes; a term usually applied to 100-percent Chardonnay Champagne or sparkling wine.

## Blanc de noirs (literally "white of blacks")

A white or slightly tinted wine made from red grapes, such as Pinot Noir and Pinot Meunier; usually applied to Champagne or sparkling wine. The tint comes from the color pigments in the red grape skins.

## Body

The weight or feeling of the wine on the palate, which can range from light to heavy or full.

## Botrytis

Botrytis cinerea is a vine disease caused by a fungus that attacks the skin of grapes in warm, misty autumn weather, effectively withering them and concentrating their juices. It is also known as "noble rot", and creates the basis for some of the best sweet and dessert wines.

## Bouquet

The smells that come from the winemaking, barrel-aging, and bottle-aging of a wine. This is different from what is meant by "aroma," which is the fruity, floral, or earthy, etc., smells that the wine gives off.

## Buttery

Often used to describe white wines (particularly those that have been oak-aged—especially Chardonnay), this term indicates a rich, creamy aroma and flavor in a wine that usually comes from a winemaking process called "malolactic fermentation." If you like this flavor in a white wine, you will want to look for wines that say they have undergone this type of fermentation.

This information may appear on the back label of the bottle.

## Character

This term describes distinct attributes of the grape variety used to make the wine. A Cabernet Sauvignon, a deep red wine, will have a totally different character from a Riesling, which is a light white wine.

## Chewy

This term is one that can cause much head-shaking and bewildered looks when non-professionals come across it. It's often used to describe big, rich red wines and indicates a dense, deep, tannic wine that has a mouth-filling texture. You wouldn't actually chew it, of course, but you might experience a definite inclination to try!

## Claret

A British term for the classic red Bordeaux blend of Bordeaux, France. In other parts of the world it sometimes refers to a red table wine.

## Clean

Used to describe a wine that lacks unpleasant aromas or tastes.

## Closed

This term is used to describe any wine that does not give off very much smell or taste. But you should make sure that it's not your cold or sinus condition that's causing the problem before you start blaming the wine! If you're sure the wine is "closed" then try aging it and/or decanting it into another, more open, container to help to open it up.

## Complex

A complimentary term used for a wine that displays layered aromas, flavors, and texture. These multiple tastes or sensations could come from the quality of the grapes used, the winemaking techniques, or its development in the bottle after some time.

## Cooked

People say a wine is cooked when it has been accidentally exposed to temperatures that are too high. A cooked wine is a spoiled wine.

## Corked wine

This is a wine that is "off-tasting" and has been ruined by moldy smells from a bad cork. The fruitiness of the wine has been diminished and the smell and taste is often described as wet cardboard or wet newspapers. Estimates are that as many as ten percent of wine bottles are "corked," which happens due to mold growing in the cork, a condition known as "cork taint." Cork, from the bark of cork trees grown in the western Mediterranean, is most often used to stop wine bottles because it is light, elastic, and impermeable to most liquids and gases. When a wine is "corked" or "corky," it is appropriate to reject the bottle in a restaurant or return it to a retail store.

## Cuvée

Literally, wine contained in a cuve, or vat. The word has several meanings, including that of a blend; in Champagne and sparkling-wine production it can also refer to wine made from a first pressing. In Burgundy, it is interchangeable with cru, or growth. It can also refer simply to a "lot" of wine.

## Delicate

Used to describe a light, soft, fresh wine, usually a white wine. To call a red wine "delicate" would not be considered praise.

## Dry

The opposite of sweet. This means the wine—whether red, white, rosé or sparkling—has little or no sugar or sweetness in it. Almost all red table wines are dry, as are many white wines. A "fruity" wine can still be dry since the term refers to fruit characteristics rather than sugar content. It is possible for the same grape variety, such as a Riesling, to be made in an off-dry, dry, or dessert wine style. The longer the grapes ripen on the vines, the higher their final sugar content will be.

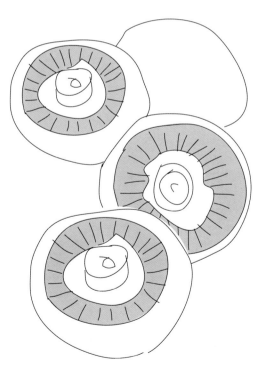

## Earthy

This term is often used to describe complex aromas and flavors detected in a wine, such as mushroom or earth.

### Enologist
The American and South African spelling of oenologist: one who studies wine and winemaking.

**Elegant!** Yes, we'd all love to be described like this—and in fact, it's a term often used to describe a wine. Actually, it's also a somewhat slippery usage, since, as with lots of things, what may be considered elegant to one person might not be to another. Generally, when using this word, wine experts are describing a well-balanced wine with a distinctive character.

### Fining
The traditional method of clarifying wine by removing microscopic elements. This is usually done through using a fining agent, which could be activated carbon or charcoal, gelatin, clay (bentonite) or egg whites—even dried fish bladders (isinglass).

### Finish
This is the final impression a wine makes in your mouth after being swallowed. It can range from short to long. Highest praise usually goes to wines with long finishes.

## Firm

Used to describe the texture and structure of a wine, usually young, tannic reds, or wines with fairly high acidity.

## Flabby/flat

A term used for characteristics of a wine lacking crisp acidity and a sturdy mouth-feel. You might use this word for a wine that has no particular structure or texture. Just as for people, this is not considered a compliment for a wine!

## Fleshy

A word you might use to describe a wine that is fatter than a "meaty wine," but is also less vigorous and more smooth in texture.

## Flinty

Often used to describe good Chablis, similar to a mineral tone.

## Full-bodied

As opposed to "flabby" or "flat," this term is used to define a wine with a rich texture that fills the mouth and has a certain weight on the palate. This is a positive and complimentary attribute and means that you are likely to enjoy a wine described like this.

## Fruit-forward

Wine writers and other experts like to use this tasting term to describe a wine that has predominant fruit flavors—usually of the grapes used to make it, but also other fruit flavors—which you notice before you note other aspects of the wine, such as acidity or tannin.

## Green

As with fruit, this term is used for wine when it shows unripe, excessively tart and sometimes harsh flavors and textures on the palate.

## Hard

This is similar to a "closed" wine and is used when a wine has a texture and structure that does not allow you to taste any flavors.

## Hot

This is used to describe a wine that has an excessively high alcohol content that "burns" the palate.

## Highly extracted

Sometimes wine writers will say that a wine is "highly extracted." What does this mean? Extract is comprised of the substances in a wine that constitute its body, flavor, and color. A highly extracted wine would be one with heavy extracts and would therefore be full-bodied, with concentrated flavors, and perhaps a dark and opaque color.

## Lean

A wine that is often high in acidity, and is lacking fruit flavors. Depending on what kind of styles you like, this could be considered praise for certain white wines, such as Sauvignon Blanc, Pinot Blanc, or Pinot Gris.

## Legs

The term comes from the fact that long, thin lines of liquid are visible inside a wine glass as it coats the glass and drips down its sides after you have swirled or tasted the wine.

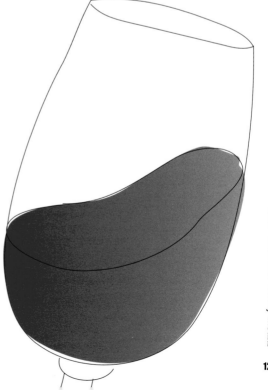

what "wine talk" really means

### Length

This refers to the finish of a wine. "Good length" means that the taste the wine leaves in the mouth lingers well after the wine has been swallowed.

### Lively

When someone describes a wine as lively, it generally means that is young, fruity, and has bright, vivacious flavors.

### Light-bodied

A wine that is delicate and pleasant, with light aromas, flavors, and texture. A good Riesling might be light-bodied, but if a Cabernet Sauvignon were so described, this would indicate a criticism of the wine.

### Malolactic fermentation

This is the conversion of the hard, apple-type malic acid in wine to the soft, milk-type lactic acid, which reduces the tart, green apple flavors and adds rich, buttery flavors. When a white wine is described as "creamy," or "buttery," it has probably gone through malolactic fermentation. This is a stylistic choice a winemaker makes. Some wines, such as many California Chardonnays, undergo this process, while others do not. It is also called "ML."

### Medium-bodied

Used to describe a wine with good weight and texture. It is less heavy than "full-bodied" but weightier than a wine that would be called "light."

### *Méthode champenoise*

The traditional method of making French Champagne. The wine undergoes two fermentations, the second one in the bottle, which creates natural carbonation and gives the wine its bubbles.

### Mousse

The term used to describe the foam on top of a glass of sparkling wine.

### Mouth-feel

This term is used to convey the impression or feel of wine in the mouth. This can be highly subjective, of course, especially when describing the tactile sensations such as "heat" from high alcohol content or "heaviness" of the liquid due to its density from high alcohol and sugar.

## Must

Unfermented grape juice, as opposed to grape skins, pips, and stalks. Called pomace in the U.S., marc in France.

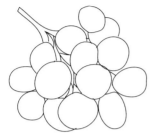

## Non-vintage

Many Champagnes or sparkling wines are non-vintage, meaning they do not bear a vintage date. Many are cuvées (see page 125), or blends, that contain wine from more than one vintage.

## Nose

This is the smell of a wine, which includes its blend of aromas and bouquet.

## Oaky

This term is used to describe the aromas and flavors contributed by oak barrels (or sometimes, oak chips) during the wine's fermentation or aging.

Oak lends such flavors or aromas as vanilla, caramel, smoke, spice or toast (the inside of every wine barrel is "toasted" with fire in varying degrees).

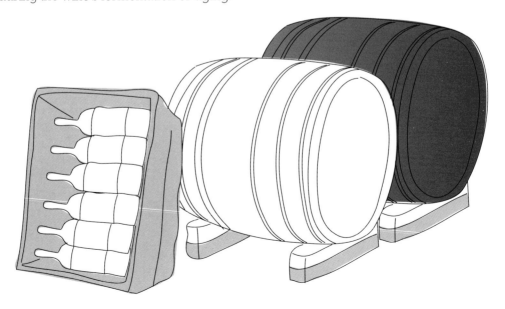

## Residual sugar

This is a technical term used to describe the amount of sugar left over in a wine after fermentation is complete. It varies widely among different types of wine. A dry table wine, such as a Cabernet Sauvignon you would drink with a steak, would have residual sugar as low as .1 or .2 percent. A dessert wine could have residual sugar as high as thirty percent.

## Oxidation

When a wine is exposed to too much oxygen, it turns brownish and takes on a cooked or baked flavor like sherry. This can occur when the wine is badly stored at fluctuating temperatures causing the wine to expand and contract and pushing the cork out. The corks loosen, exposing the wine in the bottles to oxygen. Very dry storage conditions may also cause high levels of exposure to oxygen by drying out the cork, which lets in air. An oxidized wine is spoiled.

## Phylloxera

This tiny root-eating louse damages the leaves and roots of grapevines, and was responsible for killing more than three million acres of vines in Europe in the late nineteenth century. Grafting vines onto phylloxera-resistant rootstocks is the only known way to combat this pest, and it was discovered in the late 1800s that native American vines were immune; hence most classic European vines were grafted onto American rootstocks.

### Round

A term used for a well-balanced wine showing smooth flavors and texture.

### *Sommelier*

A butler, cellarman or anyone in charge of wine. Sommeliers can also act as wine-buyers for a restaurant, and are usually highly educated about wine. Always ask their advice, as they can offer some good suggestions when you are not sure what to drink, or you are in the mood to try something new.

### Sparkling wine

The term used for any wine that contains bubbles. The opposite of still wine. Sparkling wine is called Sekt in Germany, cava in Spain, and spumante and Prosecco in Italy.

### Still wine

Any wine without bubbles.

### *Sur lie* **aging**

This French term indicates the wine has been aged "on its lees"—the term applied to dead yeast cells. The process results in greater complexity and creaminess of the finished wine. Wine not aged on its lees is clarified before aging.

### Table wine

A simple, red, white or rosé still wine that is served for day-to-day occasions.

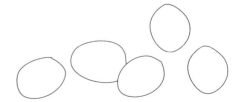

## Tannin

More often something you feel in your mouth rather than taste, but as a taste it's often bitter like the bitterness you detect in some teas or grape seeds. This is a major component of a red wine's structure and a natural preservative (also found in grapes, tea, walnuts and other foods). Tannins in wine come from grape skins, but they can also come from the oak barrels in which the wine is aged. Tannins need to be balanced with fruit; when they aren't, they leave a tactile sensation in your mouth that is felt in the middle of your tongue and sometimes described as "mouth-puckering." As a wine gets older, its tannins mellow. There is a greater tannin content in red wines than in white, which is why collectors age more red wines than white. The tannins help them develop over time.

## *Terroir*

This is a French concept in winemaking that refers to the combined effects of soil, climate, sun exposure in certain areas of vineyards, and other elements of grape-growing. It reflects the French belief that the specific place where grapes are grown is reflected in the taste of the wine. There is no exact translation in English, but winemakers in other parts of the world, such as California, also believe strongly that terroir is important.

## Thin

This is a word used to describe a wine lacking in body and flavor. It usually describes an unpleasantly watery wine.

## Toasting

This is what wine barrel-makers, or coopers, do when constructing a barrel. They heat the inside of the barrel to help the wood release flavors into a wine that will ferment in it. There can be a light, medium, or heavy toast in the barrel, which would impact on the flavors and aromas of the wine differently during barrel-aging.

## Toasty

Usually describes a pleasant aroma in wine that comes from the "toasting" over fire of oak barrels in the process of barrel-making.

## Varieties

Any grapes used to make wine. Some of the most popular are Cabernet Sauvignon, Pinot Noir, Chardonnay, Sauvignon Blanc, and Riesling, but there are hundreds. A varietal wine is named by the dominant grape from which it's made, e.g. a Chardonnay or a Riesling.

## Vegetal

When this herbal, weedy aroma and/or flavor is too strong in a wine, it can be considered unpleasant.

## Vintner

The owner of a winery and/or vineyards where wine grapes are grown. Vintner does not necessarily mean a winemaker (those who actually make the wine), though in smaller operations they may be one and the same.

## Vintage

This is the year in which the wine grapes were harvested and fermented to make a wine. The vintage is important for almost all wines since it refers to the weather conditions under which the grapes were grown. The bulk of Champagnes or sparkling wines are non-vintage because they are blends of different years.

## Vintage chart

These charts rate vintage years for wine and advise you on what was "a good year" and what was not. They can be useful in deciding what to buy, order in a restaurant, or to age—and when to drink up.

## Viticulture

The study, science, and practice of grape-growing.

## Yeasty

This attribute in a wine suggests a pleasingly fresh, dough- or biscuit-like aroma and/or flavor.

## Winemaker

The person who makes wine. He or she usually has a degree in enology or fermentation science from a college or university, but some winemakers are self-taught or learn on the job. An important part of a winemaking education is traveling to different high-quality wine regions of the world to work during their harvests and learn how grape-growing and winemaking are done in different climates and under different conditions.

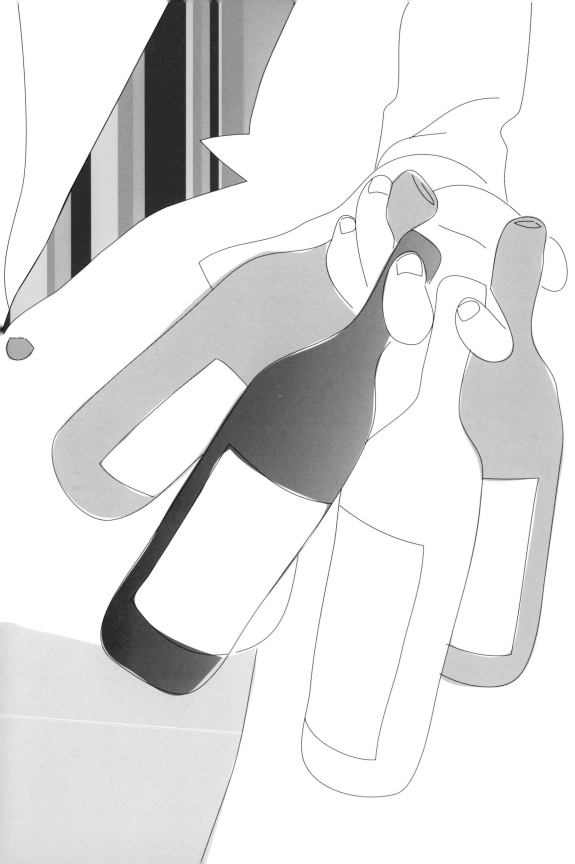

# how to serve wine

Serving wine correctly is an art in itself. Whether you're having a casual get-together with friends or a more formal wine and dinner party, you can add that extra touch of class to the occasion just by knowing how to prepare, serve and pour wine properly, using the right types of wine glasses, and gauging the correct temperature for the type of wine you are serving. All this ensures that you and your guests get the very best from every bottle. These are not trivial matters—for instance, the temperature at which a wine is served has an immense impact on its flavor. It's also useful to know how to decant wine, not just for aesthetic purposes, but also to allow the wine to breathe, and improve its flavor. As for what glasses to use, you don't have to spend a fortune on fine crystal—just choose a few basic shapes, and keep them sparkling clean, so that they enhance the delicious flavor of the wine you're enjoying.

## Acting as host

### What special gadgets do you need?

Not many. Although you could go crazy with wine paraphernalia—and you may have some fun with it—you need not buy a lot of gadgets to serve wine to guests, whether a couple of girlfriends or a party for fifty people. The essentials: wine, of course, plus wine glasses, Champagne flutes, a corkscrew, a wine bucket for chilling through the evening, a decanter if you need to decant a wine, and at least a few nibbles to complement the wine.

So, who pours the wine? Hopefully, a hired bartender. But if you're not that lucky, it's usually you or a designated friend. At a sit-down dinner party, it is supposed to be the host's job to pour the wine around the table and to make sure glasses stay filled. But do you really need to stand on such ceremony at your parties? Rules of etiquette aside, you may want to ask a friend or two, if it's a big party, to fulfill this duty so no one goes thirsty and you can attend to other details.

## How much?

Don't fill the glass too much because guests, if they want to, cannot swirl their wine if the level is too high. (See Chapter 4 for the benefits of swirling and sniffing before tasting.) It's best to fill them about one-third full to leave plenty of room in the bowl. Some people pour the wine until it reaches the widest part of the bowl, well below the rim. Remember, glasses can always be refilled—and refilled again!

## How to pour

As they do in restaurants, always try to pour the wine with the label pointing toward your guests so people can see what they are drinking. To guard against red wine drips on your light-colored tablecloth or a friend's delicate silk clothing, use "drip stops" or wine-savers: small, round, laminated paper disks stuck into the mouth of the bottle, which make any drips that form roll back into the bottle. There are also fabric-lined rings that sit around the top of the bottle to catch any wine that rolls down the side. Then there is the "twist-of-the-wrist" style of pouring in which you twist the bottle slightly as you pull it up and away from the glass you are filling. Waiters and sommeliers sometimes prefer to hold the bottle by the "punt," or indentation, at the bottom of many bottles. If you find that it makes pouring easier, do it. Practice makes perfect!

how to serve wine

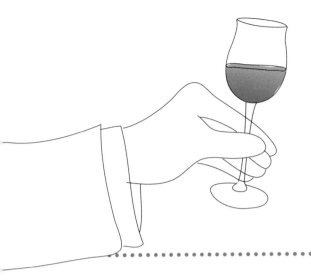

## Holding the glass

Set a good example for your guests by holding the wine glass by the stem, not by the bowl. This is not simply a wine-snob affectation; it makes good sense. If your fingertips smudge the glass, you see the wine less clearly and it looks less appetizing. If your hands touch or cup the bowl, the wine warms up from your body heat faster than you sip it.

## Set up a wine bar

Depending on how big your gathering is, set up one or more wine bars in your living room or in more than one room of your house. These can be pour-it-yourself areas and should contain everything a bartender would need to serve wine or wine drinks: several bottles of several types of wine, an ice bucket or two for the wines that should be chilled, some bottled water (still and sparkling), a corkscrew, towel, and wine glasses. Invite guests to help themselves as you greet them and remind them as the evening progresses.

## Receiving wine as a gift

It's lovely when someone gives you wine as a gift—but you have to know if it's meant to be shared. When a guest calls ahead to ask if a really special bottle he'd like to bring will go well with the menu, he is indicating that he wants the bottle opened that night—not added to your wine inventory. While this may not seem like much of a gift, if you don't mind and the wine will not clash with your food choices, you just might enjoy a new experience! Alternatively, if a guest simply hands you a bottle of wine and says, "This is for you," treat it as a gift. Put it aside to drink another night.

## Order to serve in

Just when you thought the rules couldn't get any trickier, here comes another set of them! Due to the way chemicals affect human senses, there are some guidelines to follow about the order in which you should serve and drink different wines. Generally, drink dry wines before sweet ones because the sugar will stay on your palate and affect the taste of what comes afterwards, making dry wines sour and bland-tasting in comparison. Also, drink lighter wines before heavier ones for the same reason: Full-bodied, full-flavored wines will dilute the flavors of lighter wines.

## Old before young

Young wines are usually more fruity, intense, and tannic than older wines and will overpower them when they are drunk first. As with people, maturity—and the complexity and depth that comes with it—rates over the callow young wine that will hit you over the head. Don't overwhelm your taste buds with strong flavors that will compromise your experience of the older, more rare wine.

## How to toast in any language

These are the basic toasts for drinking in several languages. May you have ample opportunity to raise your glass and use them!

**Spanish**—Salud!

**Italian**—Saluté or cin-cin!

**American and British English**—Cheers!

**French**—Santé!

**German**—Prost!

**Irish**—Slainte! (pronounced "SLAHN-jay")

**Hebrew**—Lekkhayim!

**Swedish**—Skaal! (Skøl in Norwegian)

**Japanese**—Kampai!

Research indicates that consuming more than three drinks can cause a hangover in some people while just one to two can do it to others. When you drink wine or other alcoholic beverages, your body converts alcohol into toxic by-products that may cause hangovers. There are as many hangover remedies as there are ways to overdo your drinking! Some work for some people, but not for others. There are over-the-counter products that claim to prevent the headaches and nausea of drinking too much by absorbing the toxins. There are natural remedies such as vitamin formulas, and some people swear by drinking fresh juices, Bloody Marys, and aromatherapy cocktails. But the number-one way to assure you never have a hangover is simply: Don't drink.

### Get the jump on opening

To avoid last-minute problems and scrambling, open all your wine bottles about ten to fifteen minutes before your friends arrive. This way your bottle-opening skills (or lack of them) will not be on display. You will also feel better knowing the job is done before they even walk in the door.

### Corks

Cork, which is peeled from the trunks of live cork oak trees in Portugal and Spain, has long been used to stopper wine bottles because it is effective at sealing the bottle and keeping out air. It is light, elastic, and impenetrable for most liquids and gases.

### Cork alternatives

An estimated five to ten percent of bottles are "corked," or are ruined because of faulty corks, so vintners are turning to alternative ways to seal their bottles. Among the effective and inexpensive alternatives are metal screwcaps, which require no gadget to open them, and plastic or synthetic "corks" that look and act almost the same as traditional ones but don't become tainted by cork mold.

## Cork-removal gadgets

Still, many vintners and wine-drinkers are attached to the traditional cork in the wine bottle and wouldn't think of selling or buying a bottle with anything else. They seem attached to that trademark popping of the cork when it's pulled from the bottle. The range of corkscrews available on the market attests to this. There are simple, inexpensive devices that require the user to put some muscle into the process of opening the bottle, and high-tech, high-cost models that do most of the work for you.

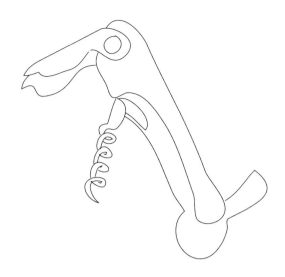

## The preferred "waiter's friend"

The original "waiter's friend" corkscrew is inexpensive and a favorite of waiters and wine servers around the world—so it must be good! It has a plated metal handle and a fold-out screw in the middle with a small knife to cut the foil capsule at the top of the bottle. At one end of the handle is a two-inch/5cm fulcrum that pulls out and extracts the cork. Watch your waiter use this corkscrew or ask him or her for a lesson next time you have the opportunity.

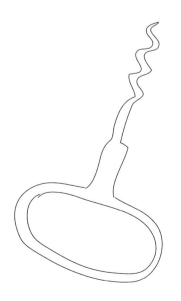

## Other corkscrews

Once you start looking, you'll find that there are many other corkscrews out there. Look for the following qualities in one you buy to use at home. Ask for one that does not have screws that are too large because they can shred the cork. Ask for one that does not push loose corks down into the bottle, such as the two-pronged "Ah-so." Ask for one that does all the work for you, if that is what you prefer, such as the winged corkscrew. The simplest model is a plastic screwpull that is small, cheap, and works very well.

### Wipe that lip!

In the case of an old wine, look to see if there is any mold on the cork before you open it. If so, wipe it away and, after removing the cork, check for any mold residue or pieces of cork left on the rim of the bottle after opening it and wipe the lip of the bottle with a damp cloth. If you are drinking a very old wine with a lead capsule, wipe away any lead residue before pouring the wine. This step really depends on the wine, and is not necessary with most of the wines you will drink.

### Fixing a broken cork

If a cork breaks off in the process of removing it from the bottle, don't worry about it. Just take the broken part out of the neck of the bottle and reinsert a corkscrew into the remaining piece. If this doesn't work and the cork falls further down the bottle or into the wine, again, don't get into a state. If it has been properly stored, the cork has been in contact with the wine for many months now and this presents no problem to the wine's taste or quality. If you do not finish the bottle, you will need to find an alternative method of closure that will keep the bottle airtight until you do. Do not allow wine remaining in the bottle to sit open for any length of time, such as overnight, or it will be ruined.

### What do you do with the cork?

Nothing, except save it to stop the bottle overnight if you don't finish it off. You may have seen people sniffing, feeling or saving a cork, but the only purposes for saving a cork is to make a cork bulletin board, trivet, or to use them to protect the sharp ends of tools or knives! Some wine experts say they can also be used to inform guests at a dinner party of what they are drinking when the wine has been removed from its bottle and decanted (see below), but the empty bottle is more effective for that because of the information on the label.

### Reinserting the cork

The best way to store wine is to replace the original cork in the bottle with a fairly tight seal, though it should not be pushed down so far in the bottle that you need a corkscrew to open it a second time. There are cans of nitrogen and various other gadgets that you can purchase to prevent wine from changing for the worse overnight. However, many of these have been found to be no more effective for a couple of days than simply stopping the bottle with its own cork.

## Screwcaps

Although it has no romance and is still an experiment, many in the wine industry say there are advantages to a screwcap over natural cork. The wine will last longer and there is no possibility of cork taint—a musty, wet cardboard taste and smell imparted to the wine when the cork goes bad. Screwcaps are being widely used in Australia, where they are said to be better at retaining fresh, fruity flavors of white wines such as Chenin Blanc, Riesling, and Gewürztraminer because of their tight seal that allows no oxygen into the bottle. Another advantage is that screwcap bottles do not need to be stored on their sides. The jury is still out, on the matter, though, because screwcaps haven't been used long enough to prove that there is good long-term aging with them.

## Opening Champagne bottles

Never use a traditional corkscrew for opening a Champagne bottle. There are gases creating pressure inside a bottle of sparkling wine and this makes the handling of these bottles a more sensitive project than opening a bottle of still wine. But it is not difficult once you try a few times and employ a few safety tips.

## How to open Champagne

Remove the outer foil at the top of the bottle and hold the bottle at a forty-five-degree angle away from you, your guests, and anything breakable or valuable. Untwist the wire cage around the cork. Hold the cork and slowly twist the bottle, not the cork, until the pressure inside the bottle pushes the cork out slowly. Ideally, you should hear a "phsst" sound, as the trapped carbon dioxide gas is released.

Here's a bit of fun—but don't try it at home! If beheading a bottle of Champagne with a sword sounds like something out of the Middle Ages, it is, but it is also practiced today with much fanfare. There is even an official brotherhood of sabering in France. Sabering is the showy way of opening a bottle of Champagne and only a few dozen people are accomplished enough to be able to do it safely. It takes slow precision, the right tools, the right bottle (some say only French Champagne bottles will work) and a bottle that has been still for a day or two. When sabered, the bottle loses its top, which flies off with the cork intact. Glass can fly, too, which is where the skill of the saberer comes in. If the bottle is not hit in the right place, it splinters.

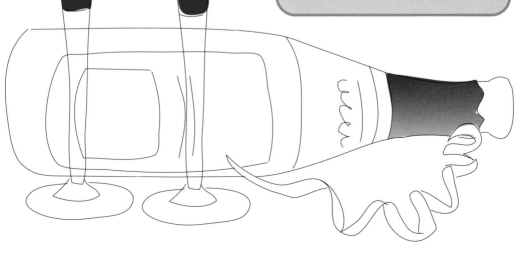

## To decant or not to decant?

You may want to decant your wines, or pour them out of their original bottles and into a glass container, for several reasons. An older wine can lose most of its sediment in the decanting process; a young, tannic red wine will soften from being exposed to oxygen or you may simply want to use that beautiful antique decanter your grandmother handed down to you. One hint: if you have guests who will care, keep the bottle around so they can see what they are drinking.

## How to decant

Decanting sounds easy but should be done carefully. If the bottle has sediment in it and your purpose in decanting is to lose the sediment (which is harmless, by the way), make sure it has been sitting upright for at least several hours, allowing the sediment to settle at the bottom. While opening the bottle, take care not to shake the contents. Make sure the decanter is not smaller than the bottle or you will be stuck with extra wine in the bottle and no place to put it. Pour the wine in one firm, continuous flow into the decanter in a well-lit area so you can watch the wine flowing out. When you see the first bit of sediment trickle into the bottle's neck, stop pouring immediately.

## Other reasons to decant

There are other practical reasons to transfer wine from its bottle to a glass carafe, such as if the bottle was already opened, maybe from earlier in the day or the night before, and you don't want your friends to think they are being served "leftover" wine, or the label has gotten wet and fallen off the bottle, or you want to have your guests taste the wine "blind." (See Chapter 4 for organizing blind tastings).

## Serving red and white together

At a dinner party, red wine may be best with one of the courses you are serving and white wine may match better with another. Or you may want to serve both a red and a white to give your friends a chance to suit their own tastes. This also gives you a chance to experiment with matching different foods and wines and to discover which combinations you like best. Ultimately, experience is what counts. You will learn more by tasting food and wine together than by following old-fashioned rules about matching food and wine. (See Chapter 9 for more advice on serving wine with food.)

## Leftover wine

Wine is a delicious beverage, and it's a shame to let it go to waste. But there are times when you've had enough to drink, and notice that there's quite a lot left over in the bottle. So when you can't manage to finish your bottle of wine during one TV football game, gossip session with your girlfriends, or dinner for two, what do you do with it? If there's only a glass or a half glass left in the bottle, you're better off pouring and enjoying it—or at least using it to cook with. Otherwise, you can preserve your leftover wine using several different methods. Firstly, always remember to replace the cork in the bottle after each pouring. Also, refrigerate leftover wine, even reds (take it out of the refrigerator thirty minutes or so before you want to drink it to take a bit of the chill off). You should also store the leftover wine in an upright position, not lay it on its side; the benefit for you and your refrigerator is that there won't be any drips to clean up. The benefit for the wine is that you are minimizing the amount of surface area exposed to oxygen.

### Squeaky clean

Make sure your glasses are spotless. This means cleaning them by hand, not in the dishwasher (they run a greater risk of breaking that way). Wash them thoroughly. Don't air dry them since spots or streaks may appear. Instead, set them upside down on a soft, thick towel to let water slide off. Then dry by hand. Make sure no soap residue is left behind to interfere with the smell of your wine. Wash glasses one at a time so they won't break in a crowded sink.

### Cleaning tools

There are special washing brushes for stemware and decanters designed to reach those hard-to-reach places where red wines sometimes leave a sticky film (or you can add a little bleach and water to the glass or decanter and let sit for a few minutes). There are also drying racks for decanters and wines glasses. Cleaning liquids specially formulated for wine glassware that cut grease, butter, olive oil, fingerprints, and lipstick are helpful, too. Their makers claim they won't etch, pit or cloud your beautiful stemware.

### Wine glasses for wine

Don't use your wineglasses for any other purposes—iced coffee or tea, parfaits or ice cream. They may look attractive when used these ways but you may never get the smells of dairy products or the cast of coffee or tea out of your glasses.

## What about Grandma's cut crystal?

The wine industry would like you to have clear glass so that you can better admire its handiwork, but the bottom line is your enjoyment. If you received cobalt-blue wine goblets at your wedding that you love, or have a special attachment to the heavy, cut-crystal goblets your grandmother handed down to you, by all means use them for wine (but you may want to use them sparingly, as lead crystal reacts with wine and releases some lead into your system every time you drink from it). Maybe you won't see the color or clarity of the wine as much, or at all, but you will probably enjoy the wine all the more because of the good feelings you get from using your most precious objects.

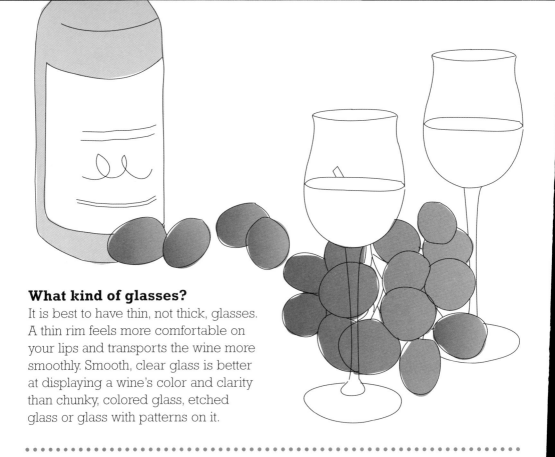

## What kind of glasses?

It is best to have thin, not thick, glasses. A thin rim feels more comfortable on your lips and transports the wine more smoothly. Smooth, clear glass is better at displaying a wine's color and clarity than chunky, colored glass, etched glass or glass with patterns on it.

## Size and shape

The shape and size of the glass can also affect the way a wine tastes. Today's makers of fine glassware claim their designs release the fullest aroma of each grape variety based on the shape of the bowl and the corresponding width of the rim. Or, they say, the shape of the glass directs the wine to certain places on the tongue and captures the bouquet, enhancing the pleasures of each wine. Usually, each glass they sell is designed for a particular type of wine, the better to enhance its bouquet and taste. Wine-glass designs are the result of thousands of years of glassmaking trial and error.

## Do you swallow it?

Many wine connoisseurs follow the theories above and invest in pricey glassware. But if you don't swallow it, or can't afford to invest in a set of fine glassware for each type of wine you are partial to, simply purchase a set of high-quality, all-purpose glasses with a capacity from eight to fourteen ounces. An all-purpose wine glass is suitable to use for serving white, red, sparkling, and dessert wines. These glasses are easily available everywhere from department to discount stores.

### Red-wine glasses

The so-called balloon shape with a rounded bowl is the most common shape of glass recommended for red wine. Because each wine has different amounts of components, such as acid, sugar, tannins, and chemical compounds, different glass shapes manipulate your experience of drinking the wines they hold. The "science" behind which shape is associated with a particular wine is more of a trial-and-error experience, but the glassware companies have done the experimentation for you. Serve Bordeaux blends, Cabernet Sauvignon, Pinot Noir, Merlot, and Zinfandel in these glasses.

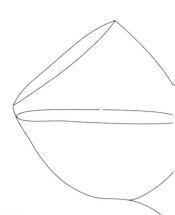

### White-wine glasses

The so-called tulip shape is the most common shape of glass used for white wine. Again, this shape has been determined to best deliver the particular weight and components of white (and also rosé) wines to your mouth. You should serve white wines such as Sauvignon Blanc, Chardonnay, Riesling, Pinot Gris, Pinot Blanc, and White Zinfandel in these.

### Champagne glasses

The de rigueur Champagne glass used to be a round, broad, shallow glass or metal cup (modeled on Marie Antoinette's breasts, the legend goes), but today's undisputed ideal for sparkling wine is a tall, narrow flute that allows the bubbles to have a nice long float all the way to the top of the glass. Serve Italian spumante or Prosecco, French Champagne, Spanish cava, sparkling wine, and German Sekt in these glasses.

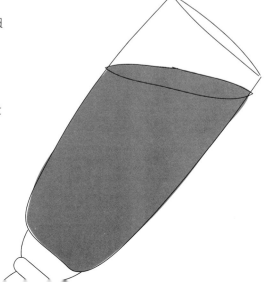

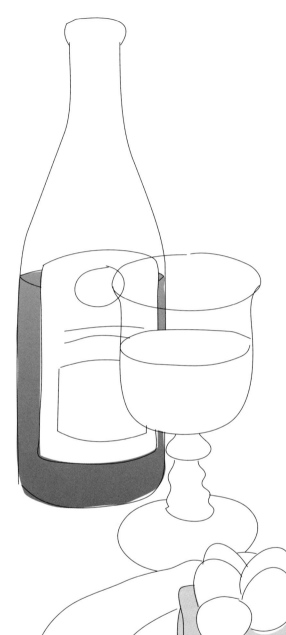

## Dessert wines

Dessert-wine glasses come in different shapes—some have tulip shapes, and some look like smaller Champagne flutes—but they are usually smaller than those used for dinner wines. There are "scientific" reasons for their design, as with any wine glass shape, but there is a practical reason, too; at the end of a meal most people tend to drink quite a bit less of a dense, rich dessert wine than they do dinner wines. Serve Auslese, ice wine, late-harvest Gewürztraminer, and Sauternes in dessert-wine glasses.

## Where on the table?

If you will have more than one wine at a dinner party and want to provide multiple glasses, the best way to arrange glasses on the table is to place them in the order they will be used from right to left. The water glass should sit farthest right above the knife.

## Why more than one glass?

It's not so common nowadays to have a different glass for every wine, but there are good reasons to do so. With two glasses, your guests won't feel obligated to finish one wine before they can have another. Also, some diners may want to compare two wines or to try both the red and the white wine with the fish course.

## How many glasses?

For large parties, plan to put out two glasses for every one guest. This is so your friends can have a clean glass should they misplace the one they were drinking from, or switch to a new glass if they've switched from drinking red to white wines, or so you can quickly and graciously provide a friend with a new glass should one break. Consider renting wine glasses from a party-supply service if you don't have enough in your own supply.

### Red-wine temperatures

The custom followed in most countries is to serve red wine at room temperature. However, current opinion in the United States says that reds are actually best enjoyed at slightly cooler than modern room temperatures. Massive, tannic red wines would be at the high end of a scale of 55° to 70°F/ 12° to 21°C, while lighter wines, such as Beaujolais, Pinot Noir, Sangiovese, and Chianti, would be at the lower end. So, to cool your red wine, you'll be putting the bottle in the refrigerator or ice bucket, if only for ten to thirty minutes.

What they say about wine temperature is true—it really does matter. Serving temperature has an important effect on what you will taste when you bring the glass to your lips; some experts say it's the most important effect. When a red wine is too warm and a white wine too cold (the most common mistakes involving temperature, which you will encounter even in fine restaurants), the wine will not taste its best. At lower temperatures, aromas are lessened and this cuts down on your enjoyment of the wine.

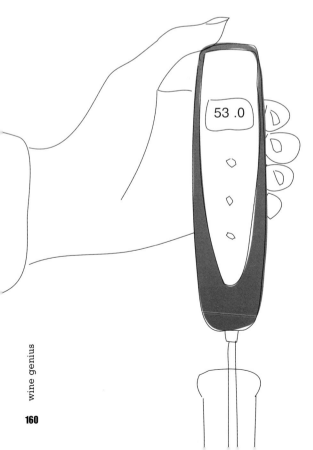

### White-wine temperatures

White wines need to be chilled, but not too much. An easy rule of thumb is thirty minutes in the freezer or one to two hours in the refrigerator. If you've had a bottle in the refrigerator for several days, take it out fifteen to thirty minutes before serving it. Sherry, Chardonnay, Meursault, and Montrachet will display more aroma, have richer flavor and better feel in the mouth at 55° to 60°F—warmer than lighter or fruitier dry whites such as Riesling, Sauvignon Blanc, Muscat, Chenin Blanc, Viognier, and Muscadet, which are best when served at 50° to 55°F.

### Dessert-wine and Champagne temperatures

Sweeter, dessert, and late-harvest wines, and all Champagnes can take the coldest temperatures of all: 45° to 55°F/6° to 12°C.

### How to gauge

So what are you supposed to do: take the temperature of a glass of wine before serving it? If gauging a wine's temperature seems tedious or daunting, use these simple rules of thumb: A red wine bottle should feel cool to the touch, but not cold. If it's too cool, leave it at room temperature for thirty minutes or so. If it's too warm refrigerate it for about thirty minutes. Serve a white wine straight from the refrigerator in warmer months. Let it sit for fifteen minutes or so in the colder months.

And believe it or not, wine thermometers do exist—even one with an alarm that goes off when the wine in the bottle reaches the desired temperature! Another type wraps a heat-sensitive cuff around the bottle and tells you the wine's temperature.

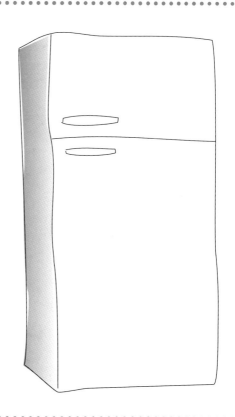

### The big chill

To chill a bottle quickly, fill a bucket with ice and water and put the bottle in it for fifteen to thirty minutes. Make sure the bottle is taking an ice-water bath; in other words, don't skimp on the water. Remove the bottle before serving, or it will continue to chill. To keep white wine chilled after removing it from the refrigerator, fill a bucket with ice and rest the bottle on top of the ice.

# chapter 8

# entertaining with wine

Entertaining guests requires thought, imagination, and a lot of forward planning. Then, when your party goes really well, you can bask in the knowledge that all your careful preparations have had a successful result. A key component in all this preparation is knowing which wines are the best choice for the occasion—whether it's a large-scale anniversary, Christmas party, graduation, or birthday celebration, an outdoor picnic, or a romantic Valentine breakfast *à deux.* You may be worried that entertaining with wine is going to be prohibitively expensive, but you shouldn't worry. Just take a look around at what's on offer. As more wine regions are opening up their treasures to the wider world, there is an amazing array of choice, and you'll find something delicious to suit a modest budget. Perhaps you'd like to throw a really different kind of event that has a "learning with fun" theme? Why not enjoy combining several pleasures by hosting a wine-tasting party. It's fun, intriguing, a great experience—and will help to deepen your appreciation of wine even more.

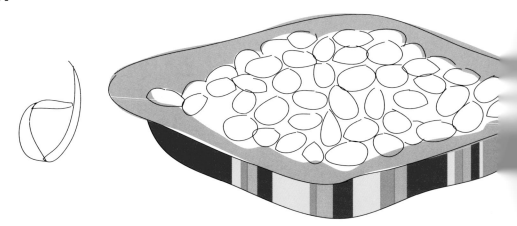

## Wine is for all occasions

Wine is a versatile beverage, as fitting for a snazzy occasion, like a fiftieth anniversary party, as it is a sentimental dinner for two old friends. It goes down nicely at a tailgate party, the most formal of dinners or a late-night tête-à-tête between girlfriends. Big, small, noisy, quiet, understated or flashy—any type of gathering can benefit from and showcase the many pleasures of wine.

## How much should I buy?

A general rule of thumb is one bottle of wine for every two people at a gathering. At a cocktail party or a mix-and-mingle party, it might be more, since typically there is less attention on the food being served and less time and fanfare taken in serving it—thus more time spent sipping. If you have ten friends coming, plan on at least five or more bottles of wine. Adjust this formula for your friends who you know will want to escape the grape and imbibe cocktails instead, or for those who don't drink much and will nurse one glass throughout the evening.

## How much at a sit-down dinner?

For a sit-down dinner, stick to the one-bottle-for-every-two-people rule, but adjust it for non-drinkers, those who might want to continue their cocktails during dinner, and also those among your guests who will stick to white (or red) throughout dinner, even though you offer different wines with different courses. And remember: In the spirit of being a generous host, it's always best to have a bottle or two extra than to be a bottle or two short.

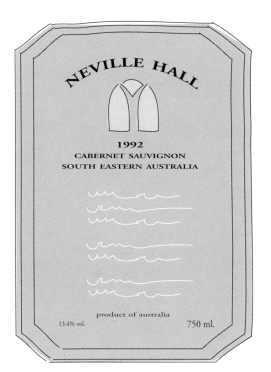

NEVILLE HALL

1992
CABERNET SAUVIGNON
SOUTH EASTERN AUSTRALIA

product of australia

13.4% vol.                                    750 ml.

## How much to spend?

In today's climate, with wine regions burgeoning throughout the world and offering competitive prices, there is no need to spend a lot of money on quality wine. Once you determine the number of guests, the amount of wine you need, and the budget for your party or occasion, you can determine how much money you can spend on wine. Again, seek the advice of a wine merchant— whether at a fine-wine store or a discount beverage warehouse—and clue him or her in on your budget. If it's on the high side, your vendor might recommend Bordeaux or Napa Valley wines. If you're watching the pennies, your best bet may be Australian or Chilean wines. Either way, you and your guests are bound to be satisfied.

## Keep your guests in mind

Your budget need not be the only sensible consideration when deciding what to spend for a party. Whether your wines come from Chile (the lower-priced end of the fine-wine scale) or Bordeaux (the upper end) might also depend on the friends you are inviting. If they are wine novices, an expensive California "cult wine" or a Mouton-Rothschild could be lost on them, and you might not get any reaction—or satisfaction—for your efforts. So keep the wine-appreciation level of your guests in mind and save the Mouton-Rothschild for a friend who'll truly appreciate it.

## Time to celebrate

Big milestones such as weddings, anniversaries, New Year parties, certain birthdays, and graduations call for festive wines. This almost always means Champagne and Champagne cocktails (*see* Chapter 10 for recipes). It may also mean special wines like Bordeaux blends or Cabernet Sauvignon that people often save and age for special celebrations and once-in-a-lifetime occasions. Or it can mean any wine you especially enjoy or your guest of honor favors.

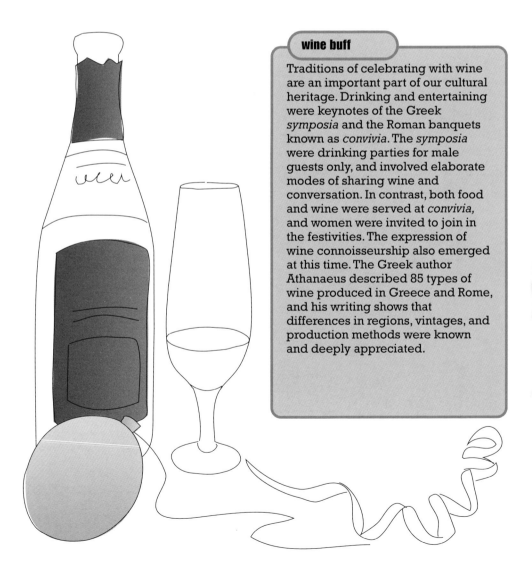

### wine buff

Traditions of celebrating with wine are an important part of our cultural heritage. Drinking and entertaining were keynotes of the Greek *symposia* and the Roman banquets known as *convivia*. The *symposia* were drinking parties for male guests only, and involved elaborate modes of sharing wine and conversation. In contrast, both food and wine were served at *convivia,* and women were invited to join in the festivities. The expression of wine connoisseurship also emerged at this time. The Greek author Athanaeus described 85 types of wine produced in Greece and Rome, and his writing shows that differences in regions, vintages, and production methods were known and deeply appreciated.

## Romantic breakfast

Morning is usually a bit too early to indulge in straight wine drinking, so the best drinks for before noon are wines or Champagnes mixed or diluted with other liquids. A traditional favorite served with breakfast or brunch in New Orleans, Louisiana, a culinary and celebration center of the United States, is a Mimosa, made of Champagne and orange juice (see Chapter 10 for details of the recipe).

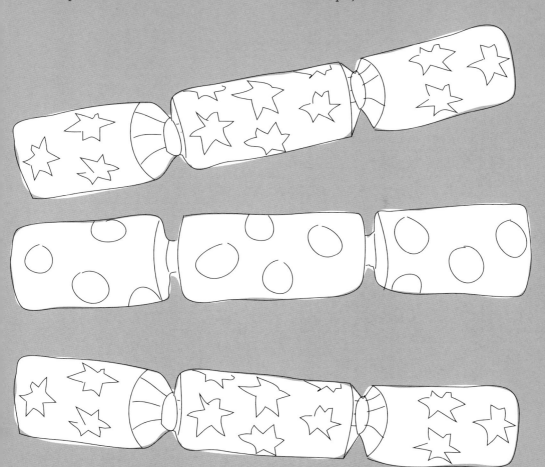

## Christmas holidays

Think pink for the holiday table. Although most often touted as summer wines, dry rosés make excellent accompaniments to a Christmas turkey dinner, New Year's ham, or the pâtés, cheeses, and breads of holiday party buffets. Rosés and pink sparkling wines, with their colors ranging from rich cranberry to pale salmon, look good on the holiday table, too. Dry rosés are made in France, other Mediterranean countries (Spain and Italy), and throughout California.

## For an evening in

Try a comforting red in winter, especially on a rainy or snowy evening. A velvety Pinot Noir can certainly do the trick, as can a Sangiovese from Italy or a spicy Syrah from California or France, or a Shiraz from Australia. These are all wines that aren't too powerful to drink alone and also go well with food. In warmer weather, a spicy Viognier, a light Riesling or a Pinot Gris can accompany everything from popcorn and a DVD to a home-cooked meal.

## Most likely to cheer you up

Champagne has both the advantage and the curse of being labeled a "special-occasion beverage." This means that many people think of it as suitable only for those few particularly celebratory times in life. Consequently, they feel excessive or indulgent if they drink it at other times. But with its effervescence, its delicate color and crisp taste, Champagne is mood-boosting. For modest budgets, try Spanish cava, German Sekt, Italian spumante and Prosecco and American and Australian sparkling wine.

## Birthdays and anniversaries

The most important thing is to make sure that that the guests of honor get to enjoy the wines they love the most. If your birthday boy is a Cabernet-lover, you might get a great bottle for the party and another as a gift for him to save. Or, if the lady adores Champagne and it's a big party serve Champagne—maybe even several different kinds.

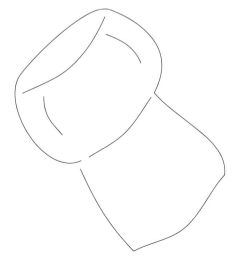

## Perfect for picnics

Warm weather inspires thoughts of picnics, barbecues, and al fresco dining. Which wine is best at these sometimes portable summer feasts? The ideal wines for casual summer repasts fall into three groups: dry rosés, fruity whites such as Viognier and Pinot Grigio, and powerful reds like Sangiovese and Rhône varieties (such as Syrah or Grenache). These full-bodied reds tend to have lots of fruit. All these wines tend to be reasonably priced, too.

## A Valentine's treat

You might want the traditional Champagne in an ice bucket for a romantic dinner for two. But for something different (or if there's no romance in your life at present), try a red-wine-and-chocolate-tasting as a Valentine's treat for you and your friends. As odd as it may sound, red wine and chocolate complement each other wonderfully, and it is delightful and illuminating to taste the way the sweetness of the chocolate softens and enhances the fruit of the red wine. First, bite into the chocolate or taste a small spoonful of chocolate syrup, and coat your mouth with it. Then take a delicious sip of red wine.

## A housewarming party

For a housewarming event, take two bottles of wine: one to add to the mix of what other guests are bringing to drink at the party and another one, preferably wrapped or with a colorful bow, to present to the host as a gift. This allows your host to put the second one aside and celebrate his housewarming later on in a quieter fashion—maybe even with you! Make sure the first bottle is something most people know and would like, such as a Chardonnay or a Merlot, and you need not spend too much on it. The second bottle will get more attention and can be a more adventurous choice, such as a wine from a faraway country or relatively unknown wine region, so spend more money and time on its selection.

## For *après ski*

When the snow has been dusted from your hair and fatigue has settled into your bones after a long day of skiing, you probably want a mellow wine like a Merlot, a Syrah or an older Cabernet Sauvignon: wines that will calm and soothe you after your workout. You might find these wines more comforting than wines that require heavy chilling, such as Champagne or fruity whites, which you might want to save for picnics and summer outdoor events.

### For summer outdoor grilling

Classic American barbecue—grilled steaks, hamburgers, chicken, and vegetables brushed with olive oil—goes well with wine. Use the same food-and-wine pairing rules you'd use at any occasion (see Chapter 9 for more details). Even in the United States, not exactly a wine culture on par with many European countries, the idea that wine is only for fancy food is outdated. So introduce wine to your backyard!

- - - - - - - - - - - - - - - - - - - - - - - - - - - - - - - - - - - - - - - - - - - - - - - - - - - - - - - - -

### Wine in moderation

Wine may be a genteel beverage, but it is important to remember it is still alcohol. Too much of a good thing (and wine is one) can still be a bad thing.

Festive occasions and special celebrations are often about excess, but you really don't want to let the alcohol consumption at your parties get out of hand and spoil the occasion.

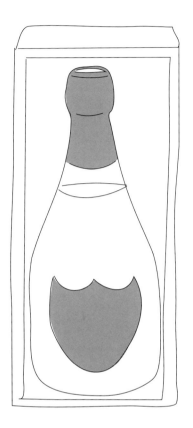

## At a business lunch or dinner

Your wine savvy, or lack of it, can help or hurt you in a business setting, too. Today, wine is considered such an integral part of business entertaining that there are extracurricular clubs and activities at the world's top business schools focused on wine tasting and education. Just as one had to play golf in times past to succeed in some fields, you now have to know how to order wine with confidence. The way you handle selecting, ordering, and drinking wine can make a significant impression on a professional colleague or a prospective boss. The day of the three-Martini lunch may be over, but the business lunch or dinner with wine is very much with us. (See Chapter 2 for details on ordering wine.)

### Hosting a wine tasting

An organized wine tasting with friends can be great fun, introducing an extra, educational dimension to getting together. Tasting wines side by side is the most effective way to learn about wines, to learn what you like best and to compare the attributes and quality of different wines. So host a wine-tasting party or suggest that a friend who's interested in wine (and has more wine glasses than you do) hosts it.

### How to organize a tasting

You organize a tasting in terms of "flights" of wine: two or more related wines. They can be related in several ways: by grape variety—three Chardonnays, for example, one from each of three different countries; or by region—three South African reds; or by producer—four Zinfandels from the same winery covering different vineyards, different vintages or different blends. Or try three Merlots, one each from three very different price categories. Be creative and organize your tasting according to what you'd like to experience.

Okay! Let's do this properly. If you want to get really purist about it, do what professional tasters do: Warn your friends not to wear perfume or aftershave (the better to smell the wines, my dear) and prohibit anyone from smoking before or during the tasting. Also, don't spray the room with air freshener or have the tasting in the kitchen where the smells of dinner still linger.

## What do you need?

Each taster should have three glasses if you are tasting three wines, four if you are tasting four, and so on. Make sure the glasses are clean and have no smell. Use a white tablecloth so you can best see the color of the wines. Have a small pad of paper and a pencil or pen next to each place setting so tasters can take notes if they want to. Things to take note of are color, smell, and taste. Encourage the tasters to share their observations.

## Tasting "blind"

The element of surprise makes the wine tasting even more fun. Pour a small amount of wine—about a third of the glass capacity—in each glass without identifying the wines. You can simply announce that the wines are all Pinot Noirs, or all from California or all rosés from European countries. Mask their identities by wrapping the bottles in small paper bags and number them or pour them into carafes (this is trickier to number—use tape—and you have to make sure you keep straight what you poured into each carafe). Pour wine number one in the first glass on the right in front of each taster, wine number two in the second, and so on. After everyone has tasted their wines and discussed them, try guessing what is what or from where. At the end, reveal their identities. You can even reward the person who has the most correct guesses (even among experts, they are usually guesses!) with a bottle of wine to take home.

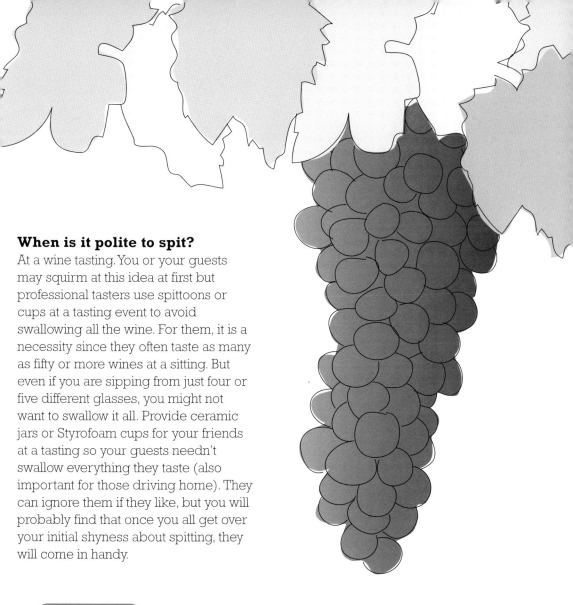

## When is it polite to spit?

At a wine tasting. You or your guests may squirm at this idea at first but professional tasters use spittoons or cups at a tasting event to avoid swallowing all the wine. For them, it is a necessity since they often taste as many as fifty or more wines at a sitting. But even if you are sipping from just four or five different glasses, you might not want to swallow it all. Provide ceramic jars or Styrofoam cups for your friends at a tasting so your guests needn't swallow everything they taste (also important for those driving home). They can ignore them if they like, but you will probably find that once you all get over your initial shyness about spitting, they will come in handy.

### wine buff

Harvard University researchers found in a study that alcohol may strengthen aspirin's apparent ability to help prevent heart attacks. The Harvard team reported that moderate drinking decreases the risk of heart attacks by increasing "good" cholesterol. But for those drinking up to one glass of alcohol per day and taking low doses of aspirin regularly there was an additional benefit: Their blood contained platelets that were less "sticky," thus avoiding internal clots that may then block arteries and trigger a heart attack. A group of other researchers in California said they found that a liter of wine contains an amount of a certain acid equivalent to almost twice the daily dose of 30mg of aspirin. They said red wine contains more of the compound than white wine.

entertaining with wine

## Taste away!

Vary the recipe for a wine tasting by having a comparative tasting of only one kind of wine. For instance you might decide to taste Spanish sherries, or ports or Champagnes. Do not worry about not having four sherry glasses per person (who does nowadays?). Use wine goblets or ask your friends to bring their own glasses, ones they will drink from throughout the evening. Since these drinks can be expensive, you could also ask each person to bring a bottle. After you've finished the wine tasting, encourage everyone to take home what is left in their bottles since all but the Champagne has a reasonable shelf life.

## Wine-tasting groups

If you and your friends have and enjoy a wine tasting, it might evolve into a wine-tasting group. Some people belong to book clubs, others to cooking clubs; wine-tasting groups are the same idea. Members of a group of friends or acquaintances rotate as hosts so everyone gets a chance. The tasting might be as often as once a month or as infrequent as twice a year, whatever works best for your schedules. Have everyone bring a bottle each time, or the alternating host could supply the wine. Tasting wine like this, in an organized fashion with input from different people, is the best way to learn about it.

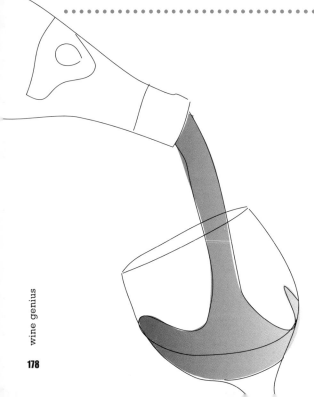

## Wine and cheese: instant party

You want to get together with a group of friends, have a bonding session with your work colleagues, or throw a housewarming party. But time is short. The easiest recipe for this is a wine-and-cheese-party, since everything can be bought (wine, cheese, bread, crackers, fruit) and nothing needs to be cooked. One way to organize such a party is to pair each cheese with a wine from the same country or region the cheese comes from: for example, a French Roquefort with a white burgundy, a Spanish Manchego with a Tempranillo or a California Chardonnay with a Sonoma goat cheese.

## Get friends involved

Get your friends involved by asking each to bring either a bottle of wine or a different cheese. For friends without a clue (we all have them!) give them specific instructions on which wine or cheese to bring so you don't end up with "cheese" in a spray can. If you want to leave it up to their discretion, pass onto them that wine and cooking professionals generally believe that white wines go better with cheese than do reds. Try including a bottle of red in your party to see if you agree.

## Fond of fondue?

Another take on the classic wine and cheese party is to melt the cheese—à la fondue. Throw a fondue party in the winter when the wind, rain or snow outside makes the warm, melted cheese all the more inviting and comforting. Cheese fondue can be made from scratch by melting grated cheese and adding garlic, finely chopped onions and mushrooms, and a splash of white wine, but it's easier still to buy prepared fondue in the refrigerated section of the grocery store and simply heat it on the stove top, then transfer to a fondue pot lit by a simple tea light. Supply bread, small boiled potatoes with their skins on, blanched vegetables, and apples and pears for dipping. Supply small fondue forks with long handles for each guest.

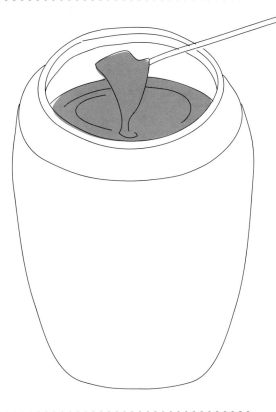

## Dessert party

After a movie, play or concert, invite your friends back to your place for a luxurious spread of desserts. Again, everything can be purchased at a bakery or grocery store or made by you ahead of time. As in any repast and any occasion, wine can play a starring role. Sauternes, late-harvest dessert wines, port, and Champagne are all appropriate and delicious with an array of desserts from dense, rich chocolate tortes to lighter fruit desserts. Include a cheese plate, too, and don't forget the coffee and tea.

entertaining with wine

## Spring brunch

Host a spring brunch at the first sign of sunny weather. In addition to breakfast items, serve light-lunch items including quiche or frittata, salads, chilled marinated asparagus spears, crudités, and a fresh-fruit salad. Chilled Champagne, mimosas, a light white wine such as a Riesling and/or a rosé would all work well with most brunch items. Provide sparkling water for those who might like to mix it, or alternate it, with their wine.

## Wine and hors d'oeuvres party

People lead busy lives, so having a classic "cocktail" party when you don't feel like hosting a dinner or you and some friends are going to a concert or a play later in the evening makes sense. Serving wine instead of cocktails means no preparation or mixing so you can enjoy the party instead of playing bartender. This also encourages people to meet each other since no one is stuck next to only a few others for the duration of the meal. All your friends can meet each other more easily.

## Setting it up

Serve a selection of wines with a selection of finger foods you can buy, make or heat up from a frozen state. If you serve enough finger foods and some of them are hearty fare, they can serve as a dinner substitute. Set up a wine bar or two (include water bottles, soda, and ice at these) and food tables so you do not have to serve all night. Start passing hot hors d'oeuvres when half of your guests have arrived and replace them often. Also serve several kinds of cold hors d'oeuvres that won't need your attention after being set out.

## Wines for a multi-course dinner party

You can serve different wines with different courses at a dinner party. If your meal has three courses and you will have three wines, make sure you have three glasses for each person. (Borrow from friends if you don't have enough or rent wine glasses for the evening from a party service.) The table should be set with the three glasses plus a glass for water at the beginning of the meal. Pour each glass one-third full, introducing the new wine as you serve each course. Don't have all three glasses already poured when your friends sit down to dinner. Leave the bottles on view so people can see what they are drinking and can help themselves to more, unless you are acting as pourer, or a designated friend is. (For advice on what wines to serve with your courses, see Chapter 9 on food-and-wine matching.)

# pairing wine with food

Are some wine and food partnerships truly made in heaven?
Well, yes—some are. Strawberries and Champagne are a perfect
example, and the classic combination of Muscadet and *moules
marinières* really do seem made for each other. So, it's often a
good idea to pay attention to established tradition, as well as
learning to explore your own taste preferences. This will give you
the confidence to experiment, and the knowledge of when to
ignore mainstream recommendations. Most people will tell you
that you should drink red wine with red meat—but try serving a
young, fruity red with roast chicken, and you'll soon discover how
quickly that rule is disproved. You'll find it's a great combination.
As a useful rule of thumb, pair sweet wine with sweet food, acidic
wine with acidic or salty food, spicy wine with spicy
food, red wine with red meat and white wine with white—that
way, you'll always be safe.

## Red with meat

Have you heard the one about drinking red wine with meat and white wine with fish or chicken? Who hasn't? These days, though, it's a bit of an outmoded idea, since white wines and red wines of different styles can often be enjoyed quite nicely with the same dish (roasted chicken is a perfect example). The bottom line is that you should drink the wines you enjoy most with the foods you like best, regardless of color. So why worry at all about what wine goes with what food? Well, both wine and food are complex substances with taste elements in them that can be altered depending on what you're combining in the same bite. So there are quite a few legitimate considerations when pairing wine with food that will considerably heighten your enjoyment of both.

## Light vs. heavy

If there is one rule to keep in mind about pairing wine with food, it is that lighter wines go better with lighter foods and heavier, full-bodied wines go better with richer, heartier cuisine. Drink a light white wine like a Riesling or a Pinot Grigio or a light red wine like a Pinot Noir with a light dish like pasta primavera. (But beware: Not all Pinot Noirs are light!) The point is that a delicate white wine that would go well with a delicate seafood dish such as Coquilles St. Jacques would be overwhelmed by a slab of cow. If you love White Zinfandel, but want to have prime rib for dinner, try having your White Zin as an aperitif and have a glass of (or a sip of your boyfriend's) heartier red, such as a Syrah or a Merlot, with your beef. Start with this notion when choosing a wine for your food—or when choosing the food to go with the wine you'd like to drink.

## Simple vs. complicated

Another rule some people like, and one that may make sense to you, is one about complexity. The more complicated the flavors in the food, the simpler the wine. For example, a New Orleans-style gumbo with lots of different ingredients, spices, and flavors is best paired with a young red wine, not an old Cabernet Sauvignon revealing layer upon layer of flavors (although most experts agree that beer is the best partner for this dish). Instead, save that old Cabernet for a flavorful cheese, simple crackers or nuts, or even to drink alone. Remember: Rules are meant to be broken. Experiment and try different combinations.

## Look to its origins

Another useful general rule in pairing food with wines is to look to the region where your food or wine comes from and pair accordingly. Pair a southern Italian red wine with a seafood dish from southern Italy. Pair a Sancerre or Sauvignon Blanc with a classic French preparation of seafood, such as fruits de mer. Match a strong cheese from Greece with a Greek wine or grape variety that came from Greece. The idea is that these recipes and wines grew up together, so to speak, and were probably adapted to each other over time, so they are a safe choice. You may find this rule too restrictive or impossible to follow, but when in doubt, it's a useful notion to keep in mind.

## Does wine go best with French food?

If you followed the "origins" rule above, you might conclude that wine goes best with French food. Although the earliest-known history of wine places it in the Middle East, the French have been the world leaders in wine production and know-how for hundreds of years. They serve it (diluted) to their babies and use it as medicine. Following the "origins" theory, wine has evolved in the French culture alongside French food, so they would be uniquely suitable for each other. But even the French would say that their wines are compatible with everything from American hamburgers to Brazilian fish stew. Wine is made from so many different grapes, in so many sites around the world, in so many different climates, in so many styles, and is perceived so differently based on circumstances, that it can be suitable for almost any cuisine.

## Rich foods

Red wines pair well with fat-rich foods, such as different cuts of beef, because of the wine's tannins—the same thing that preserves the wine and allows it to age. So do crisp, dry Champagnes—their acidity cuts through the super-rich tastes of liver pâté, foie gras or deep-fried foods.

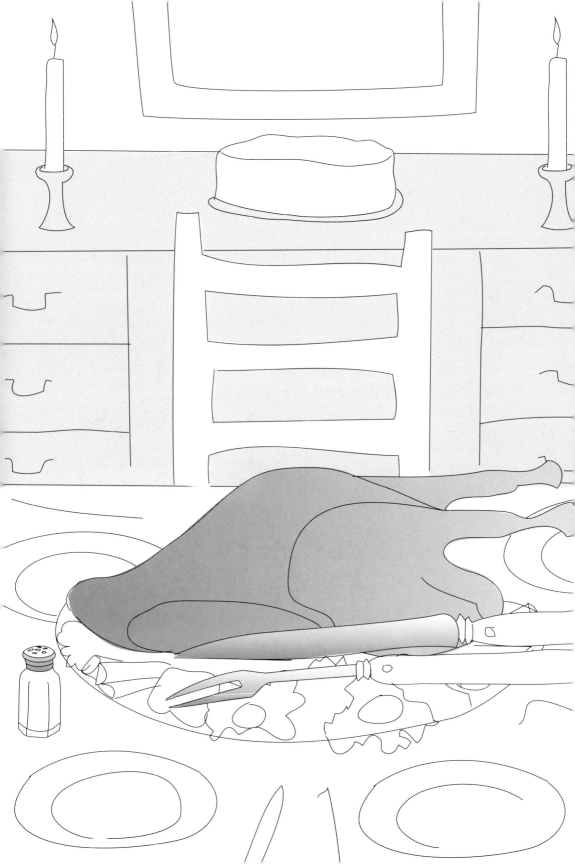

## If you're attuned to the seasons

You may want to think of wines as "seasonal" in the same way that foods are. Pinot Noir goes well with lamb and mint for spring. Chardonnay is a summer wine that pairs well with the foods of summer, such as fresh fruits and vegetables. Deep and rich Zinfandel goes well with the heartier foods we veer toward as the weather turns cool in fall (and is often touted as perfect with turkey for Thanksgiving dinner). And for winter, sparkling wine takes center stage at holiday parties and occasions, but also pairs well with the rich, comforting foods of winter such as mushrooms.

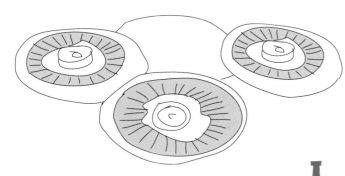

## Low-fat delight

Wine could be considered a diet food. If you're on a low-fat diet, rejoice! Wine is fat-free. If you're on a low-calorie diet, consider that wine contains only about eighty to 100 calories in a four-ounce glass, and lighter wines can have fewer calories than heavier ones. If you're on a low-carbohydrate diet, dry white wine has minimal carbohydrates—under one gram in a four-ounce serving and only two grams for the same amount of red wine. Beware of off-dry (slightly sweet) and sweet dessert wines, though, which are high in carbohydrates because of their high sugar content. For example, a glass of dry white wine may have one gram of carbohydrate while a very sweet dessert wine could have up to thirteen grams. And for heart health, wine is fine because it is cholesterol-free, and it also helps reduce the plaque that sticks to artery walls.

I've got to bring in a dieter's caveat here. Many in the wine industry, especially when selling aperitifs or sparkling wines, often refer to wines as "appetite stimulants"—an odd claim if you think about it. With obesity on the rise in today's world, there are few people who would seem to need to stimulate their appetites! But this very characteristic may be harmful to the dieter. For even though wine has no fat or cholesterol and minimal calories and carbs, many people report that drinking wine or other alcohol lessens their resolve about dieting. So while the wine itself may not add calories, carbs or fat, it may lead to eating more foods that do.

## What *doesn't* go with wine?

Any combination you don't like! Wine, though a versatile, elegant, and delicious beverage, doesn't always hit the spot for all people. Don't feel forced to drink or serve wine at every fancy occasion or with every food you serve. Wine experts and writers will tell you that wine goes with everything from borscht to wild boar, but don't always believe it! Here are a few foods that you may find wine doesn't match terribly well: pickles, vinegar, asparagus, celery, candy, ice cream, cookies, cream cheese, peanut butter, and popcorn.

## Use wine in your cooking

What would a hearty spaghetti sauce be without a dash of a robust red wine? Or Coquilles St. Jacques without the addition of dry vermouth? Or a creamy cheese fondue without a splash of white wine? Wine adds great flavor to your cooking and is not complicated to use in many dishes. It's as simple as adding a splash of sherry or Madeira to your homemade chicken or turkey gravy or adding ¼ cup of dry red wine to spaghetti sauces, stews, and many hearty Italian dishes such as chicken cacciatore. Steam mussels and clams in a mixture of white wine and water, and poach scallops and salmon in a poaching liquid of dry white wine or vermouth, water, spices and other flavorings, such as carrots and celery. You needn't be a gourmet cook or a cooking-school graduate to get really creative with wine.

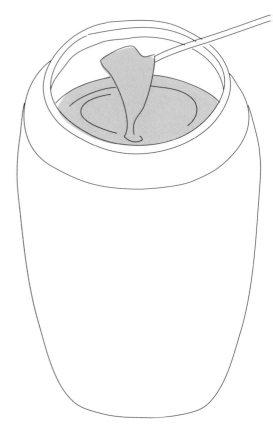

## What to buy for cooking

The wine industry will tell you to never use any type of wine in cooking that you would not drink straight, but that is overzealous advice based on wanting, as in any business, to sell as much of its product as possible. Instead, let common sense guide you. Using an entire bottle of very expensive red wine for "drunken pork" (in which pork marinates overnight in the wine, which is then discarded) or a high-end white burgundy to steam clams or mussels is a waste and an unnecessary drain on your budget. On the other hand, if you only need one-third of a cup of wine for your recipe and want to drink the rest of the bottle with the meal, it might make sense. Don't buy cheap, so-called "cooking wines" in the grocery store,

because the quality and taste will not do justice to your culinary efforts. But feel free to buy at the lower end of the price scale when searching for a bottle that you will use primarily in a recipe—as long as you stick to known quality wines. After all, you may want to finish off the bottle after you've used what you need in your recipe. The wine should be good enough for that!

## When you're cooking with *and* drinking it

When your recipe calls for wine and you're also going to serve wine with the meal, choose the same type of wine to serve. That doesn't mean the same bottle because it makes more sense to spend more on the wine you will drink. But you still want compatibility between the wine in your dish (especially if there is a lot of wine in it, such as in coq au vin) and the wine you will drink along with it. So serve a Zinfandel at the table if you are putting Zinfandel in your coq au vin. By the way, most recipes will simply call for a "dry red wine" or an "off-dry white wine," in which case feel free to choose a wine within that category that suits your taste and budget.

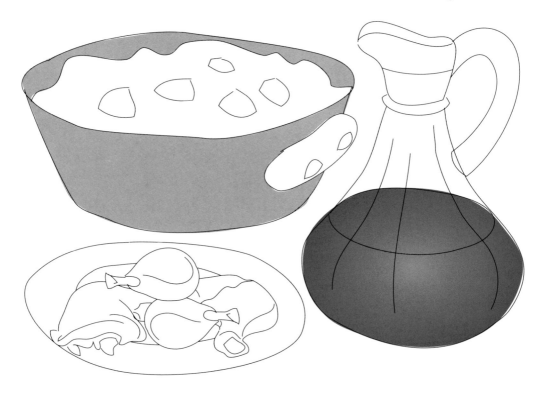

### wine buff

It's widely thought that cooking destroys alcohol. Not all the alcohol in wine burns off in the cooking process. In some dishes, where you add wine at the end and stop cooking it altogether or continue to cook it only for a short time, most of the alcohol will remain in the dish. If you're simmering wine in a sauce or stew for a long time—say, an hour or more—most of it will evaporate. Keep this in mind when you're cooking for your friends who are non-drinkers or may be sensitive or allergic to wine.

## In a restaurant

When you want to order a certain dish but have an inkling your favorite wine will be too subtle or overpowering with it, seek the advice of the server or sommelier, if there is one. Describe the kind of wines you like and then explain your food choice. Since servers or sommeliers should be familiar with the ingredients in various dishes on the menu, they should be able to come up with suitable suggestions, and you can expand your horizons by trying a new wine or a new combination of food and wine. If a new wine you've never tasted is suggested and you're not sure about ordering it, ask for a small taste. (See Chapter 2 for food-pairing suggestions listed by wine types.)

## What wine nuts do

True wine aficionados look forward to a restaurant experience more for the wine than for the food. They may consult the wine list first in a restaurant, studying it for as long as twenty minutes before deciding what they want to drink. Then, they check the menu for what best complements the wine they've chosen, usually choosing rich, flavorful foods to go with rich, flavorful wines or subtly spiced foods to go with light, delicate wines.

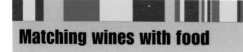

### Chicken

Wines that go well with chicken dishes depend on what's in the dish. Heavier wines, usually reds, would go well with a hearty chicken *cacciatore* (containing spices, tomatoes, and other vegetables) while a light red wine, such as Pinot Noir, a light white, such as Sauvignon Blanc or a dry rosé would go well with plain roasted chicken. Chardonnay, a light red wine or a fruity Viognier goes well with a smokier-tasting grilled chicken or chicken with a fruity sauce.

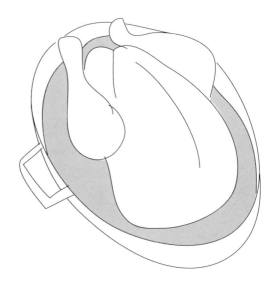

### Beef

Again, to choose a wine for beef you must consider how the beef is prepared. If it's a plain, juicy steak or a slab of prime rib, a robust wine such as a Cabernet Sauvignon, Zinfandel, Syrah or Bordeaux blend would stand up to it and help cut the fat that will coat your mouth. For an Italian dish that contains beef but also flavorful ingredients like garlic, tomatoes, olives or cheese, try an Italian red, California Zinfandel, Cabernet Sauvignon or Merlot, or a Shiraz from Australia. Cabernet Sauvignon and Syrah (Shiraz) go with a variety of grilled red meats and stews. Merlot is ideal with winter stews and hamburgers. Cabernet also matches well with heavier meat dishes such as sausages and beef-and-bean dishes. Sausages and ribs also go well with Zinfandel.

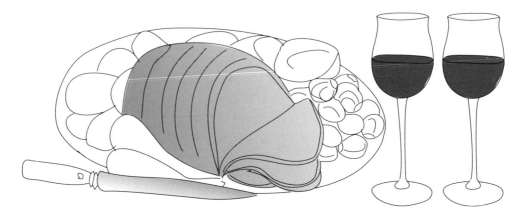

wine genius

## Other meats

Pinot Noir, one of the most food-friendly of all wines, is compatible with pork, duck, lamb, venison, and wild game, although many people prefer heartier, powerful reds with the last four meats; try Napa Cabernet, Rhône reds, or Australian Shiraz. For a roast lamb with garlic, olive oil, and other pungent Mediterranean flavors, try Italian wines, Zinfandels, Cabernet Sauvignon or Merlot. A Pfalz Spätlese or Riesling grand cru also drinks well with a light meat, such as pork or squab, but make sure the sauce or accompaniments aren't too strongly flavored.

## Fish

Sauvignon Blanc (Sancerre in France) complements lighter fish dishes such as shrimp, crab, lobster, Petrale or Dover sole, and halibut. Chardonnay, generally richer than Sauvignon Blanc, goes well with richer fish or fish preparations such as grilled salmon, shrimp scampi, and Lobster Newburg or lightly spiced fish dishes. Pinot Noir also pairs well with salmon, and Merlot works with tuna and swordfish.

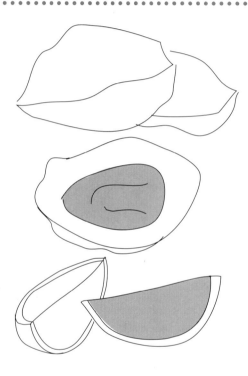

## Oysters

Why a tip on matching wine with oysters? Because there's at least one major competition dedicated to the subject each year. And raw oysters, with their pure, briny taste of the sea, combined with a crisp white wine is a sublime combination. At the Pacific Coast Oyster Wine Competition, an annual contest to identify a group of wines that can be recommended as good "oyster wines," the wines chosen as best paired with oysters on the half-shell are usually Sauvignon Blanc (or French Sancerre), dry Chenin Blanc (or French Vouvray), and Pinot Gris. Other excellent choices are Muscadet, Chablis, and dry Riesling.

### wine buff

The most difficult grape to handle is Pinot Noir. Winemakers describe it as thin-skinned and unforgiving, fickle in the vineyard, tricky in the winery, and definitely a challenge. It insists on well-drained soils and warm temperatures moderated by fog or cooling breezes from the sea, but at the same time it is susceptible to mold and mildew. And it can't be beaten up like the thicker-skinned Cabernet Sauvignon; it must be handled gently. The best Pinot Noirs from Europe come from the Burgundy region of France, while the best American Pinot Noir comes from Oregon and California's Russian River Valley.

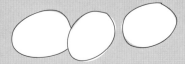

## Pasta

All pastas have basically the same taste so you need to concentrate on how a pasta dish is sauced to best match it with a wine. Is it light or heavy? If it's a delicate olive oil and/or butter sauce with a hint of garlic and parsley, drink a Pinot Grigio or other light white wine or a light red. If it's a hearty sauce packed with vegetables and meat, go for a Sangiovese, a Tuscan blend, a Chianti, or a Zinfandel.

### wine buff

Some of the highest alcohol wines in the world are Amarones from northern Italy. These are massive wines that stand up to hearty stews, game, and roasts and they typically have an alcohol content of fifteen percent or higher (most dry dinner wines have alcohol contents of around ten to twelve percent). Since the 1990s, many California Zinfandels have been made to pack a punch, too—they are even beating Amarone with alcohol levels approaching sixteen percent.

### Snack foods

Champagne with potato chips? Yes! The salt and oil of the chips is a perfect contrast to the crisp acid of a dry Champagne. Light, crisp sparkling wines usually contain fresh, fruity flavors that refresh and cleanse the taste buds when eating salty, creamy or nutty foods, so instead of saving the bubbles only for special occasions, think of it for your casual snacks, too. Pizza is great with many red wines—Sangiovese, Chianti, Cabernet Sauvignon, Merlot— and some whites such as Pinot Gris and Chardonnay. Salted nuts and olives go with just about anything light and young, such as Merlot, Chardonnay or Pinot Grigio. Sherry is always served with little dishes of salted almonds, olives, and other tapas in Spain.

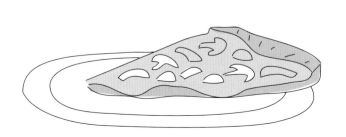

## Japanese food

The Japanese would say sake (rice wine) goes best with Japanese food, but the western world has found that sparkling wine is a perfect match for sushi and sashimi (delicate raw fish slices without the vinegared rice). Because of its subtle flavors, it will not overwhelm the subtle taste of the fish, and its high acid content will tame the fire of the green horseradish (wasabi) and ginger slices that accompany it. Pinot Grigio or Sauvignon Blanc would go well with raw fish, too. Deep-fried shrimp, chicken, or vegetable tempura would also match well with sparkling wine. For the sweet-salty flavors of teriyaki chicken or beef, try Cabernet Sauvignon, Merlot or a Bordeaux blend.

## Salads

Matching salads with wines can be tricky because of the vinegar in most salad dressings. If you can substitute lemon juice for the vinegar in your salad dressing, you can avoid the clash of flavors that results from wine and vinegar. Creamy salad dressings are another answer, allowing you to choose freely what wine you drink. But watch out for particularly bitter salad greens, such as arugula or radicchio, which can clash with wines. Choose a wine high in acidity, such as a Sancerre (Sauvignon Blanc).

## Desserts

That's easy: the classic dessert wines. Sauternes, late-harvest wines, port, and Champagne all go well with certain desserts. Also, port and chocolate are an amazingly good match and many dessert wines are a good partner to lighter, fruit desserts.

## Do dessert wines seem like too much?

Even many people who are devoted wine-drinkers say enough is enough and often turn up their noses at dessert wines by the end of a meal. They may feel they have had too much alcohol, too many calories, or that the sweetness of the dessert wines is too much for them combined with the sweetness of the dessert they're eating. If that's the case with you, feel free to forgo a port or a late-harvest wine at the end of the meal. Or, you might want to try the dessert wine instead of dessert, since both of them are sweet.

• • • • • • • • • • • • • • • • • • • • • • • • • • • • • • • • • • • • • • • • • • • • • • • • • • • •

## Wine and chocolate

Here's a surprising combination: Cabernet Sauvignon with chocolate. For those who normally regard a full-bodied Cabernet Sauvignon as too robust or harsh for their taste buds, the chocolate is a perfect antidote. The sweetness of the chocolate softens and enhances the red wine and brings out its yummy fruit. First, bite into the chocolate or taste a small spoonful of chocolate syrup, and coat your mouth with it. Then take a sip of red wine. You'll be surprised at what you experience.

## Vegetarian cuisine

Vegetarian diets are increasing in popularity, and even non-vegetarians eat more salad, bread, and vegetables in a typical meal than they do an entrée of meat, poultry or fish. So it is surprising that more attention does not get paid to pairing wine with vegetables and vegetarian cuisine. Wine can go beautifully with vegetables, cheese, breads, and other side dishes or staples of a meat-free diet.

## Light vs. heavy

We're back to the light and heavy rule. Pair a heavy wine like Cabernet Sauvignon with robust, starchy vegetables such as fresh corn or roasted potatoes, and they will bring out the fruit in the wine. A stuffed artichoke or roasted vegetables with olive oil will also go well with a Cabernet Sauvignon because the roasted quality of the vegetables complements the darker tones of the Cabernet. The same wine would work well with a hearty vegetarian lasagne.

## Compare and contrast

A crisp Sauvignon Blanc or Chardonnay matches well with a cream soup such as sweet corn or cream of mushroom. A fruity white wine could also provide an interesting contrast to the creamy texture of an artichoke. Pair fruity, bright wines such as Sauvignon Blanc, or an Italian red Sangiovese, with vegetables that have bright flavors such as tomatoes, asparagus, and green beans.

## Go rustic

Earthier wines go well with rustic foods such as grilled potatoes, red peppers, and olives. Cabernet Sauvignon can work well with bean dishes and strong cheeses. Provençal reds, such as Bandol, or Italian Sangiovese are nice with a rustic, whole-wheat olive bread or something similar. A Zinfandel would work well with savory dishes that include berries or fruits to bring out the wine's jam characteristics. And Merlot goes well with a vegetarian pizza.

# chapter 10

# wine
# drink
# recipes

With a few standby bottles of wine and other simple ingredients, you can produce the most delicious array of drinks in no time at all. Rather than falling back on the same old spirits and tonic formula, give your guests a treat with a choice of stunning sangria concoctions; and woo your beloved with breakfast in bed and a Mimosa cocktail made from Champagne. Once you've tried making a few drinks based on wine, you'll be delighted to discover just how versatile they can be. Whether it's a sparkling summer punch for a party crowd, or an exquisite glass of kir royale for one, you'll prove that you have the imagination and style to put it all together. These particular recipes are created to make the most of wine—which also means buying the best bottle that you can afford. Just because you are adding other ingredients, you won't disguise the thin flavor of a badly made product. So, go on! Explore what's on offer, pull a few corks, and enjoy being really creative with wine.

## Taking stock

A little forward planning makes sense. Even if it's only a humble corner of your kitchen or pantry, set aside an area in your home that's stocked with the things you need to whip up wine or Champagne cocktails, punches, or other drinks. It won't be a big undertaking to entertain some drop-in friends or to throw a last-minute get-together if you are well prepared. Have on hand at all times a couple of bottles each of red and white still wine and Champagne. Add a bottle each of Cognac and/or sherry if you like.

## What else?

Not much else is needed that probably wouldn't be in your kitchen anyway. Some fruit juice, such as orange or cranberry, sparkling water or club soda, lemon-lime soda, a jar of maraschino cherries, a lemon, lime and/or orange, sugar, and grapes or strawberries for a pretty garnish. What might not be on your weekly shopping list are little plastic or bamboo skewers—useful for spearing garnishes and "decorating" your drinks. Also stock some liqueurs you like (cassis, the blackcurrant liqueur used in kir and kir royale, is especially useful).

## Convenience foods

Handy snack foods to have on hand that are appropriate and delicious with the drinks that follow in this chapter are easy to buy and keep around until needed. Roasted and salted nuts, olives, cheeses, canned peppers, and other antipasto items are a snap to take from the cupboard or refrigerator, open, and serve. Place them on pretty dishes around the room where people will be sitting and voilá: instant party!

## Be creative

The recipes that follow are delicious and fun, and you should try as many as sound good to you, but let them guide you to new discoveries if you like. At your next get-together, stage a contest among your guests to see who can come up with the best wine- or Champagne-based drink from the few ingredients you supply (these are listed above). Reward the triumphant winner with a delicious homemade treat or a bottle of wine or Champagne.

wine drink recipes

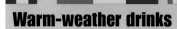
# Marimar's Sangria

This is an authentic recipe from the Spanish region of Catalonia.

**3 bottles full-bodied, dry red wine**
**2 large lemons, sliced thinly, with peel cut in one long spiral**
**2 large oranges, sliced thinly, with peel cut in one large spiral**
**2 large peaches cut into slices**
**3 tablespoons sugar, or more to taste**
**½ cup/125 ml brandy**

**½ cup/125 ml orange liqueur**
**¼ cup/60 ml gin**
**Any additional fruits, such as strawberries and grapes (not melon, which will discolor)**
**2 or 3 x 10-ounce/300 ml bottles of club soda**
**Ice-cubes**

**1** Place all ingredients, except club soda and ice-cubes, in a large glass punch bowl or pitcher. Stir well. Taste to adjust ingredients if necessary. Cover and refrigerate at least 4 hours.

**2** At the last minute, add club soda and ice. If you make it 6 hours ahead or more, add fruit shortly before serving so the fruit doesn't get mushy and discolored. Serves 12 people or more.

I love making sangria, especially in the summer. It's such a happy drink and is perfect with spicy food or Mediterranean dishes. And if you're having a barbecue, this a great drink to accompany food off the grill. Sangria is highly versatile, also: You can vary the red wine depending on what food you're cooking—use a lighter wine with seafood, something fruitier with chicken and poultry, and a robust red with beef and other strongly flavored dishes. Make sure all of your ingredients are well chilled, as sangria is best very cold. A really cool tip is to serve it with ice cubes made from wine. so that the flavor of your delicious sangria does not get diluted by melting ice.

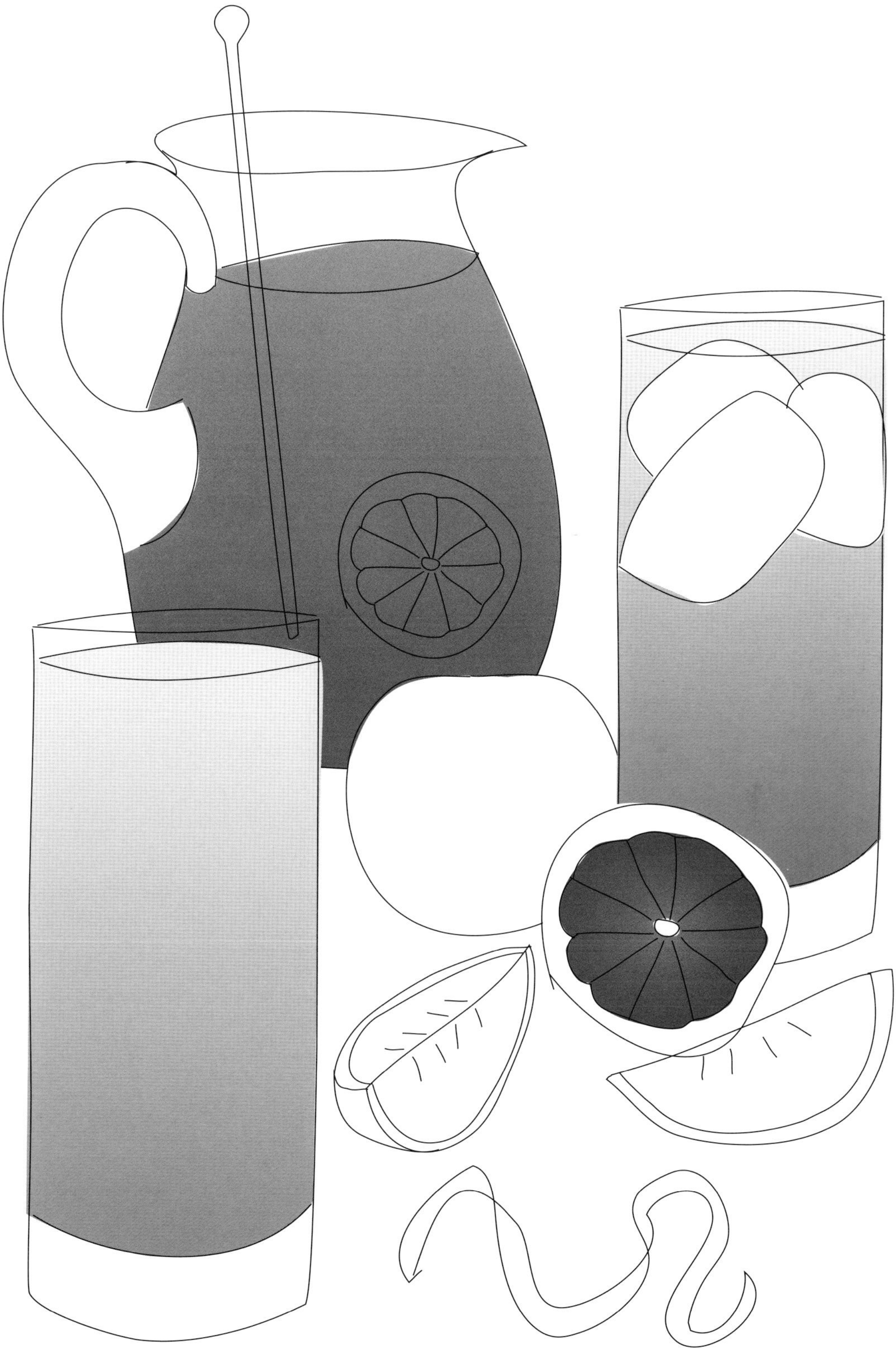

# Red Sangria

2 bottles of a dry, fruity red wine, such
as Zinfandel or Merlot
2 cups/475 ml cranberry juice
3 cups/750 ml orange juice, preferably
freshly squeezed

20 fresh strawberries, cleaned and
speared in twos on small plastic or
bamboo skewers
Large bottle of lemon-lime soda

**1** Pour wine and juices into a glass
pitcher or punch bowl. Stir well and
then whisk.

**2** Pour ⅔ full into tulip-shaped wine
glasses, old-fashioned glasses or glass
punch cups filled with ice.

**3** Top with speared strawberries and
soda. Makes 20 servings.

# White Sangria

2 bottles dry white wine, such as
Chardonnay or Sauvignon Blanc
4 cups/1 liter grapefruit juice,
preferably freshly squeezed

30 white (green) grapes, washed and
speared in threes on small plastic or
bamboo skewers

**1** Pour wine and juice into a glass
pitcher or punch bowl. Stir well and
then whisk.

**2** Pour ⅔ full into tulip-shaped wine
glasses, old-fashioned glasses or glass
punch cups filled with ice

**3** Top with speared strawberries and
soda. Makes 20 servings.

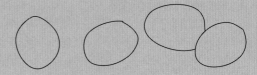

# Spritzers

These are light, refreshing, festive drinks without all the alcohol of a straight glass of wine.

| | |
|---|---|
| Red still wine, or white still wine | Ice |
| Club soda or sparkling water, chilled | Garnish of cherry or lemon, lime or orange peel |

**1** Take any kind of glass you want and simply add chilled club soda or sparkling water to the red wine, white wine or brandy in the proportion you want. (Try half-and-half to start with, and then adjust according to your taste and mood.)

**2** Add ice and a speared cherry or twist of lemon, lime or orange.

# Kir

In France, this is used as a cold remedy!

| |
|---|
| 1 teaspoon of cassis (blackcurrant liqueur) or Chambord (raspberry liqueur) |
| 5 ounces/150 ml of dry white wine, chilled |
| Lemon twist |

**1** Mix cassis or Chambord with the wine in a tulip-shaped wine glass or Martini glass.

**2** Garnish with lemon twist, and serve. Makes one drink.

Fruity *Crème de cassis* is a sweet, intense, black currant-flavored liqueur which transforms an ordinary glass of white wine into a delicious summer drink. This classic liqueur dates back to 16th-century France, and kir is a hugely popular drink all over the country.

# Wine Cosmopolitan

A wine twist on the popular cocktail.

2 ounces/60 ml Cabernet Sauvignon
1½ ounces/45 ml cranberry juice
½ ounce/15 ml vodka

½ ounce/15 ml Cointreau
Lime twist and grape, for garnish

**1** Shake all ingredients with ice and strain into a chilled Martini glass.

**2** Garnish with lime twist and grape on a small plastic or bamboo skewer. Makes one drink.

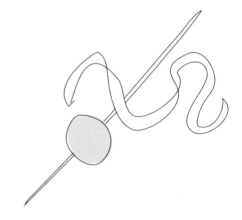

# The White Zintini

2 ounces/60 ml White Zinfandel, very cold
1 ounce/30 ml vodka

Lime wedge and maraschino cherry, for garnish

**1** Chill a Martini glass. In a shaker, pour the White Zinfandel and vodka over ice. Stir, don't shake!

**2** Pour through strainer into a Martini glass and garnish with a lime wedge and a maraschino cherry. This makes one drink.

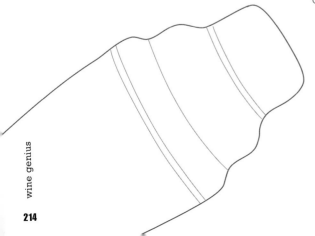

# The Chardonnay Power Cooler

For those days by the pool when you want something low-alcohol, refreshing, caffeinated, and low-calorie.

**3 ounces/90 ml Chardonnay** | **Diet lemon-lime soda**

**1** Pour the Chardonnay over ice in a tall, preferably frosted, glass

**2** Top with diet lemon-lime soda. Makes one drink.

# The Red Bishop

A weekend brunch pick-me-up.

**3 oz/90 ml red wine** | **½ teaspoon superfine sugar**
**1 oz/30 ml lemon juice** | **Thin slices of orange, for garnish**
**12 oz/360 ml orange juice** |

**1** Combine wine, lemon juice, orange juice, and sugar in a cocktail shaker half-filled with ice-cubes. Shake well.

**2** Fill a highball or wine glass with ice-cubes and strain into the mixture into the glass.

**3** Garnish with orange slice. Makes 1 or 2, depending on size of glass used.

# Mimosa

A great Sunday or vacation brunch drink.

**1 part orange juice, preferably freshly squeezed**  |  **2 parts dry Champagne**
**thin orange slice, for garnish**

**1** Combine Champagne and orange juice in a Champagne flute or tulip-shaped wine glass and stir.

**2** Garnish with the orange slice and serve. Makes one drink.

# Bellini #1

A refreshing concoction that hails from Italy.

**3 parts dry Champagne** | **1 part peach schnapps**

Combine the Champagne with the
schnapps in a Champagne flute or
wine glass and stir. Makes one drink.

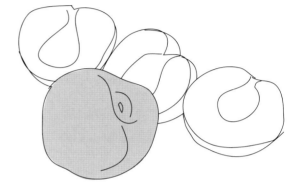

# Bellini #2

**Dry Champagne** | **orange twist**
**1 teaspoon peach liqueur** |

Pour the peach liqueur in a flute or Martini glass; fill with Champagne. Toss in the
orange twist. Makes one drink.

# Bellini #3

**Dry Champagne**
**Purée of fresh peaches, refrigerated**
**or frozen**

Scoop a few tablespoons of the fresh-peach mixture into a cocktail glass or
Champagne flute, top with Champagne, and stir. Makes one drink.

# French 75

2 ½ ounces/75 ml gin
2 ½ ounces/75 ml freshly squeezed
lemon or lime juice

2 tablespoons superfine sugar
**Dry Champagne**
**Lemon or lime zest**

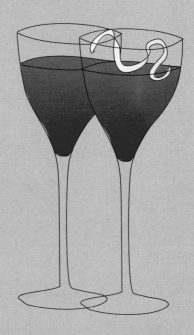

**1** Combine gin, fruit juice, and sugar in a cocktail shaker or blender and mix. Pour into 2 Champagne flutes or wine glasses and top with Champagne.

**2** Garnish with lemon or lime twist. Serves 2.

# Kir Royale

1 teaspoon of cassis (blackcurrant
liqueur) or Chambord
(raspberry liqueur)

5 ounces/150 ml of dry Champagne,
chilled
**Lemon twist**

**1** Mix in a Champagne flute or Martini glass with Champagne.

**2** Garnish with lemon twist. This recipe makes one drink.

# Ambrosia

A citrus-fruit love potion that combines brandy and Champagne.

| | |
|---|---|
| 1 ounce/30 ml brandy | ½ ounce/15 ml orange liqueur |
| 1 ½ teaspoons lemon juice | ⅓ cup/85 ml chilled Champagne |
| ½ ounce/15 ml triple sec | |

**1** Mix all ingredients except Champagne in a tall flute or an old-fashioned glass.

**2** Add ice and top with Champagne. Makes one drink.

# Chandon Fizz

This refreshing fizz is a citrus-bourbon mix with a kick, from the famous French Champagne house.

| | |
|---|---|
| 1 ounce/30 ml Bourbon | 4 ½ ounces/135 ml dry Champagne |
| ½ ounce/15 ml orange juice | orange peel, for garnish |

Combine in a Martini glass, garnish with orange peel, and serve. Makes one drink.

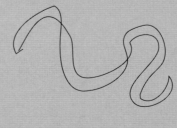

# Chandon Cocktail

This is a fruity, sparkling-wine punch.

| | |
|---|---|
| **2 bottles dry Champagne** | **4 cups/1 liter crushed ice** |
| **2 x 12-ounce/350 ml cans club soda** | **6 ounces/180 ml frozen limeade** |
| **2 x 12-ounce/350 ml cans ginger ale** | **6 ounces/180 ml orange juice** |

**1** In a large punch bowl, mix orange juice and limeade concentrates.

**2** Gently stir in sodas, add Champagne, and serve in a rocks glass over crushed ice. Serves about 20.

# Tropical Punch for 30

For a summer celebration.

| | |
|---|---|
| 1 ripe pineapple | 4 oz/120 ml Cointreau or Triple Sec (or |
| 2 cups/600 ml fresh lemon juice | other orange liqueur) |
| 1 scant cup/200 g superfine sugar | 2 oz/60 ml brandy |
| 2 bottles Champagne | 1 quart/950 ml club soda |
| 1 bottle dry, white wine | 4 cups/1 kg mixed fruits, fresh or froze |

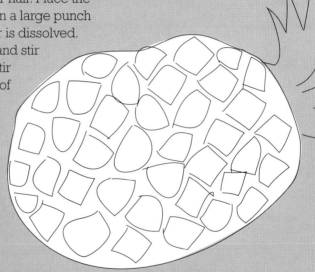

Chop half of the pineapple very finely, and thinly slice the other half. Place the lemon juice and sugar in a large punch bowl and stir until sugar is dissolved. Add remaining liquids and stir well. Add the fruit and stir well. Add a large block of ice to the punch bowl before serving. Makes 30 x 6-oz punch cups.

# A Night in Paris

| | |
|---|---|
| 2 tablespoons French Cognac | Lemon zest twist |
| Dry Champagne | |

**1** Pour Cognac in bottom of Champagne flute, top with Champagne and stir lightly.

**2** Add twist of lemon zest to glass and serve. Makes one drink.

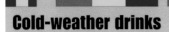
# Hot Mulled Wine

Usually a treat around the end-of-year holidays, this warming beverage can be equally enjoyable on ski trips and other wintry evenings and outings. You can sometimes buy the ready-made spice bag for hot mulled wine in a gourmet food store and simply combine it with a bottle of dry red wine simmering in a pot on the stove.

| | |
|---|---|
| **2 bottles fruity but dry red wine** | **1 ½ teaspoons grated nutmeg** |
| **4 oranges, peeled and sliced thinly** | **1 ½ teaspoons allspice** |
| **(reserve peel)** | **3 cinnamon sticks** |
| **8 whole cloves** | **½ cup/100 g granulated sugar** |
| **1 ½ teaspoons ground mace** | **2 cups/475 ml water** |

**1** In a large non-aluminum saucepan, boil the water together with the orange peel, cloves, mace, nutmeg, allspice, cinnamon sticks, and sugar. Heat on high and stir frequently to dissolve sugar. Bring to a boil, then reduce heat to a simmer over medium heat for about 10 minutes.

**2** Strain the mixture and return the liquid to the saucepan. Add the wine and warm it gently, but do not allow to boil. Serve in individual glasses with a slice of orange peel in each. This serves 12 to 15 people.

# Witch's Brew (from Spain)

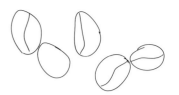

This is an authentic recipe that hails from Galicia, Spain.

**6 tablespoons sugar**
**2 cups/475 ml grappa or brandy,**
**preferably Spanish**
**2 cups/475 ml dry red wine**
**Peel of 1 large lemon**

**1 large Pippin or Golden Delicious**
**apple, peeled, cored, and cut**
**into wedges**
**1 tablespoon coffee beans**

**1** In a heavy-bottomed skillet, dissolve sugar in 1 or 2 tablespoons of water and cook over medium-high heat until sugar caramelizes and turns brown. Add grappa or brandy (it will hiss, but do not worry), and scrape with a spatula to dissolve the caramel. In a separate pot, heat the wine.

**2** Transfer the caramel-brandy mixture to a flameproof container that you will be serving from (a round, shallow clay casserole is traditional). Add the lemon peel, apple, and coffee beans.

**3** Take the casserole or other dish to the table immediately, so the brandy stays hot, and ignite with a match and flambé. Now, turn off the lights and evoke the witches! When you have had enough of a show, douse the flames with the hot red wine. Serve warm in small cups or glasses. Serves about 8.

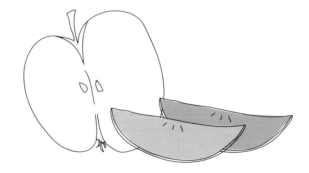

# Chandon Holiday

**2 parts dry Champagne**

**1 part eggnog, whipped frothy,**
**if desired**

Pour into a Martini glass, Champagne flute or tulip-shaped wine glass and stir. Garnish with a small plastic spear containing a red cherry and a green cherry. Makes one drink.

# chapter 11

# the world's wine regions

Nowadays, drinking wine is like going on a world trip without leaving home. Never before has so much wine, in such variety, been exported from so many countries on such a scale. It is simply awesome. We are now living in a golden age of winemaking. Just take a stroll along the shelves of your local wine store, and check out all the different places where each wine was made. Then you'll realize the sheer scale of what the world's wine regions have to offer you. And that's immensely exciting. You can sample the best wines from regions as far apart as Australia and Argentina, Chile and Spain, California and Bordeaux, often at prices that are easily affordable. Moreover, travel companies have already zeroed in on the preferences of wine lovers, and offer tours to wine-producing regions everywhere, with trips to wineries and wine tastings included as part of the package. It's when you're traveling that you'll truly appreciate drinking local wines and brews with the local cuisine. They have evolved together and are usually uniquely suited to one another.

## Classifying French wines

There is also a complicated system of classifying the wines based on quality. In Bordeaux, for instance, the 150-year-old system of rating wine estates put in place by a group of wine merchants even varies from one region within Bordeaux to another. These top wines are the *crus classés*, or "classified growths." *Premiers crus*, or "first growths," are the top classified wines, the most prestigious and pricey. There are also *deuxièmes crus* ("second growths," etc., all the way to fifth growths. There are also *premier-* and *grand-cru* vineyards in Burgundy (for Chablis, for example).

Don't be confused by French wines, with unfamiliar names. Here's what you need to know: In France, wines are not named or classified by their grape varieties, as so-called "New World" wines are (i.e. those from North America, Australia, New Zealand, South America, and South Africa.) So, just when you've learned to differentiate a Pinot Noir from a Pinot Gris, you'll find it of no help when reading a French wine label. French wines are named sometimes by the geographical areas where they come from (Bordeaux, Burgundy, Rhône) and often by even more specific regions and *appellations contrôlées* (official classifications) within those areas.

## Know your terminology

*Château* wines are French wines produced by a wine producer who owns a *château*. The word originally meant "castle" or "big house", but today, what it really means is the kind of winery that has vineyards and/or a wine-making facility on the property. Yet far from the grandeur that the word suggests, the facility and building could be quite modest. The Bordeaux region has the most, but not the only, *châteaux*, and wines made by, say, Château Margaux and Château Lafite are among the world's most revered. These days, however, many wine producers in France (and all over the world, including the United States) have tacked the title *"chateau"* onto their names—the better to sell wines.

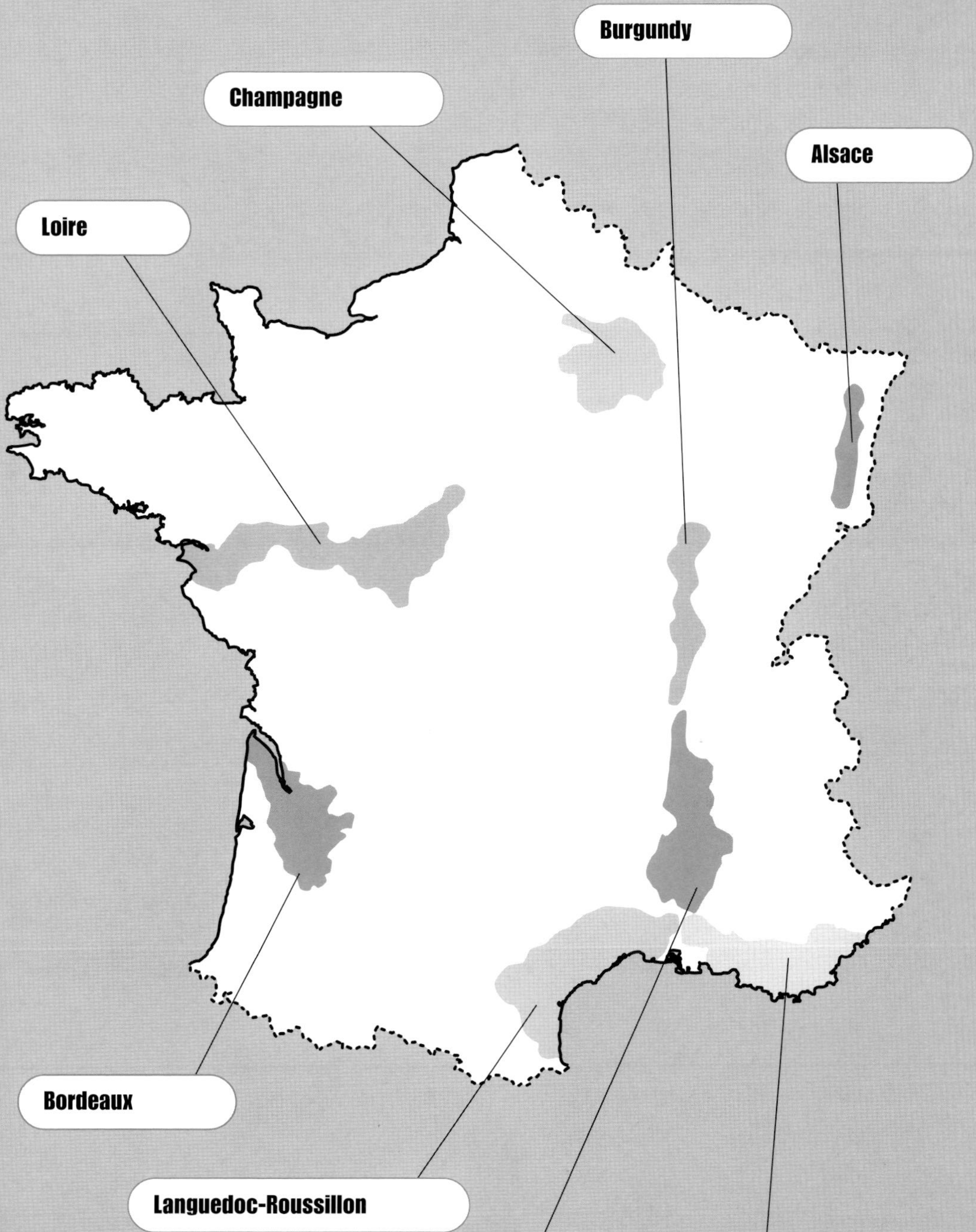

Burgundy

Champagne

Alsace

Loire

Bordeaux

Languedoc-Roussillon

Rhône

Provence

## Above board in Bordeaux

Visit Bordeaux because it is considered one of the best wine regions in the world and buy Bordeaux wines because they are known for their finesse and high quality. Nobody does it like the French, and Bordeaux, located in southwest France, is the most famous fine-wine region in the world. Bordeaux's reds are usually based on Cabernet Sauvignon and Merlot, but almost all are blends, including other varieties such as Malbec, Cabernet Franc, and Petit Verdot. Good Bordeaux rouge is crisp, herbal, and cedary, with blackberry and blackcurrant flavours. The Bordeaux region also turns out Sauternes, one of the most famous dessert wines. Most Bordeaux wines are expensive and highly prized by collectors because they age for a long time. Top areas include Margaux, Pauillac, Pomerol, and St-Emilion. Lesser known but still good wine regions within Bordeaux include Puisseguin St-Emilion, Blaye, and Lalande de Pomerol.

## Burgundy

Buyer beware: Burgundy is known for its expensive wines, complex Chardonnays and Pinot Noirs that are often cited as the best of their kind in the world. You might get hooked! Whereas most white wines should be drunk within two to three years, white burgundies with their multi-layered flavors, can age for five years or more as they develop deeper aromas and flavors. Top areas within Burgundy include Chablis, the Côte de Nuits, and the Côte de Beaune. A wine-drinker could suffer a migraine trying to figure out the intricate classification system of wines in Burgundy; indeed, deciphering Burgundy is like trying to make rocket science simple! The highest-quality level of wine, and most expensive, from Burgundy is the grand cru. The lowest is a Bourgogne (red or white), but many wines at this level are well worth trying and provide good value for money.

## Roaming the Rhône

If the venerable Bordeaux and Burgundy regions seem a bit too much like the wines mother or even grandmother might prefer, try France's Rhône region for something a little more trendy. Grenache, Syrah, Mourvédre, Cinsault, and Carignan are the main varieties produced in this region, located in the south of France, near Provence. The highest-quality wines, ones that are rich-tasting, high in alcohol, and loaded with fruit, are from Châteauneuf-du-Pape and Gigondas in the southern Rhône. Wines from the Côtes du Rhône can be good buys and are generally drunk young, not aged. In the northern Rhône, Côte-Rôtie and Hermitage are known for their steep hillside vineyards that grow Syrah, a spicy red (although whites are produced as well).

## Alsace

Head for the Alsace region of France or Alsatian wines in your wine store if you are a white-wine fan. Mostly a white-wine region in northeastern France, Alsace produces Pinot Blanc, Tokay-Pinot Gris, Riesling, Muscat, Chasselas, and Gewurztraminer (here spelled without the ü), and only a little of one red wine, Pinot Noir. The region also makes some sweet dessert wines, and its sparkling wine is called Crémant d'Alsace. The highest-quality wines are classified as grand cru. As opposed to most white wines, several white wines from Alsace, including Pinot Gris and Riesling, can age well.

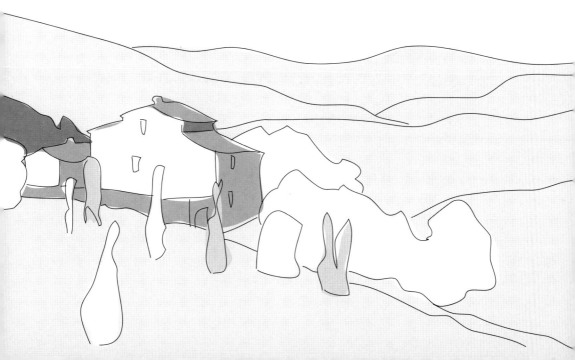

## Lounging in the Loire

Visit the Loire in central France if you want an easy, laid-back wine country weekend while visiting Paris. And if you like crisp, dry white wines from the Chenin Blanc, Sauvignon Blanc, and Muscadet grapes, Loire wines will tickle your fancy. Not quite on a par with Burgundy or Bordeaux, the Loire region is still a desirable area for French wine production. The best-known wines are from the Vouvray, Sancerre, and Pouilly-Fumé appellations within the Loire region. Rosé d'Anjou is also a wine to watch. The Loire is also France's second-largest area of sparkling-wine production, next to Champagne.

## Languedoc-Roussillon

Try the so-called Rhône varieties from the Languedoc-Roussillon, France's most up-and-coming wine region. Value, dynamism, and excitement—this area has it all. Once the source of ordinary table wines, the Languedoc is the largest wine-producing area in France and offers reasonably priced Chardonnay, Merlot, and Sauvignon Blanc (often called by their grape variety names—unusual in France) and new, high-quality Rhône wines made from Grenache, Mourvédre, Carignan, and Syrah grapes by a band of devoted artisan winemakers with ambitions to build this area a higher profile. Some of the best wines come from Faugères, Pic St-Loup, and the Coteaux du Languedoc.

## Champagne

If you really love Champagne, then why not go to the source? Legendary around the world as the birthplace of the wine world's most festive product, Champagne is located in northern France and is one of the world's coolest winemaking regions. Champagne from Champagne is about traditions dating back to the seventeenth century, and it is made using the same three grapes—Chardonnay, Pinot Noir, and Pinot Meunier—sometimes as a blend of two or all three of these, sometimes as 100 percent Chardonnay (*blanc de blancs*). It is always made in the same way, using the *méthode champenoise*, or Champagne method, which was developed here. Two fermentations, instead of the single fermentation that still wine undergoes, take place and it's the second one that gives it those tiny bubbles. Champagne can age, but most people prefer to drink it young while it still has a lively kick to it. It also makes great cocktails (*see* Chapter 10).

## You've read about it, now taste it: Provence

Head for Provence—or a wine store—to try the area's dry rosés. An area known more for its bewitching ambience than its wine, this region in southern France, sprinkled with medieval hill towns against a backdrop of green countryside, underwent a change after enjoying its time in the international literary limelight in the 1990s. As in most of France, wine has been made here for hundreds of years, but it was lackluster. Now, the quality has improved. The area, especially Lubéron, is providing tourist-friendly tours and tastings to visitors and there is even a corkscrew museum. Wines here are also pleasantly affordable.

## Italy

**wine buff**

You might say (especially if you're Italian) that Italians like and know their wines more than anyone else in the world. That's because Italy makes more wine than any other country and its people rank third in consumption per capita. There are wine-growing regions all over "the boot" and on its principal islands, and the intricacies of Italy's wine regions are notorious for their complexity. Italy has experienced a rebirth of its winemaking since the 1990s. There are a striking variety of wines made here—from the enigmatic and expensive "Super Tuscans," (*see* page 234) to a wide variety of respectable table wines that won't break the bank. Barbera, Nebbiolo, Dolcetto, Montepulciano, and Sangiovese are Italy's most common and popular red grapes used, and Pinot Grigio is the best-known white.

## Piedmont: head of the class

Choose the mighty Barolo and Barbaresco wines that hail from the Nebbiolo grape and are made in Piedmont if you want rich, powerful wines. Among the highest in the hierarchy of Italian wines, wines from the Piedmont region of northwest Italy also include Barbera, "the people's wine," which goes down easier than most wines made from Nebbiolo. Dolcetto is another easy-drinking red made here. Among dry whites, the most common and highly favored is Arneis, followed by Favorita. Piedmont is also known for Asti, a sweet-ish sparkler.

## Tuscany: not just Chianti

Experience Tuscany for yourself, either in person or, if you're not that lucky, then in a glass of its most emblematic grape, the Sangiovese. In central Italy's bucolic countryside, Tuscany is widely considered one of the prime winemaking regions of the world. Dotted with ancient olive trees, old vines on rolling hills of green velvet and medieval villages, it is also considered one of the best wine regions to visit. This is the home of Chianti, that wine-in-a-basket that everyone knows from Italian restaurants, and it is also home to the "Super Tuscan" and to high-quality red wines with long names that at first seem impossible to pronounce, like Brunello di Montalcino and Vino Nobile di Montepulciano. Dry white wines made here come from the Trebbiano grape, although the finest are almost all made from Chardonnay these days.

wine genius

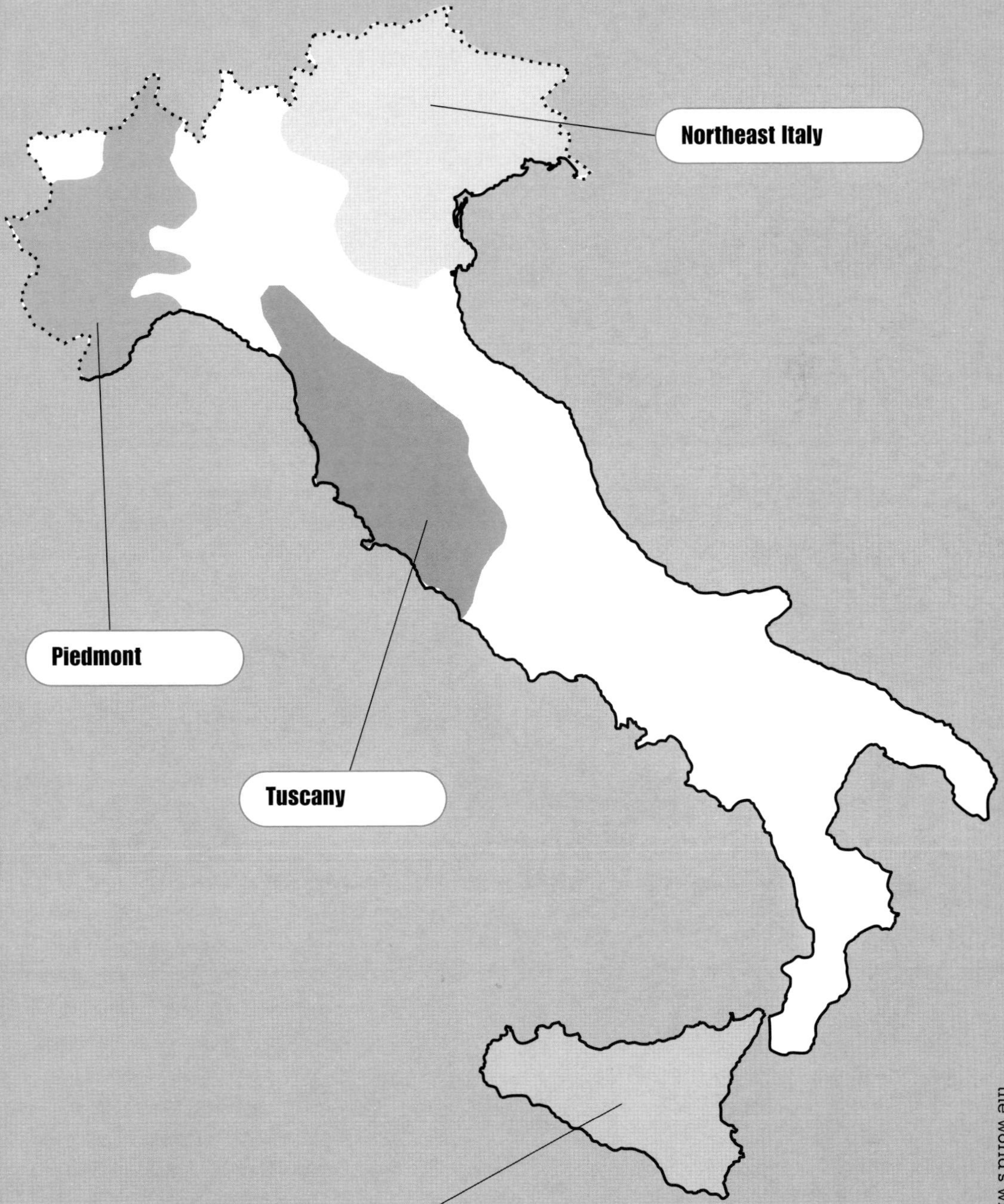

Northeast Italy

Piedmont

Tuscany

Sicily

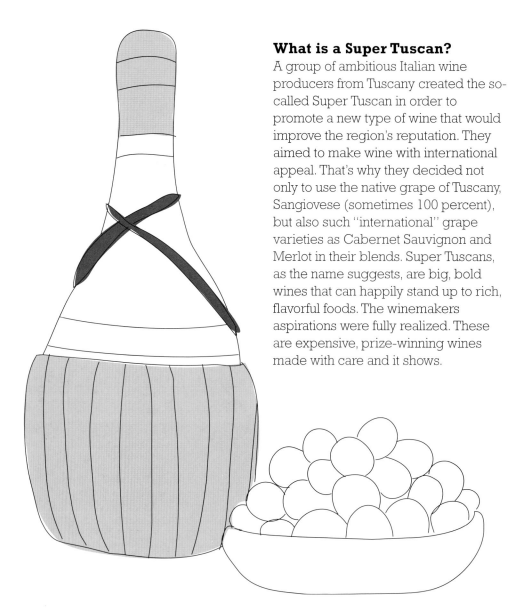

## What is a Super Tuscan?

A group of ambitious Italian wine producers from Tuscany created the so-called Super Tuscan in order to promote a new type of wine that would improve the region's reputation. They aimed to make wine with international appeal. That's why they decided not only to use the native grape of Tuscany, Sangiovese (sometimes 100 percent), but also such "international" grape varieties as Cabernet Sauvignon and Merlot in their blends. Super Tuscans, as the name suggests, are big, bold wines that can happily stand up to rich, flavorful foods. The winemakers aspirations were fully realized. These are expensive, prize-winning wines made with care and it shows.

## Sicily

If you're a true Marsala fan, you should look for the sweet, fortified wine from Sicily—the most well-known of the island's wine products. Sicily is one of the top dessert-wine regions in Italy. It used to make standard bulk wine, but the prolific wine industry housed on the island that looks as though it's being kicked by Italy's boot, has undergone a big change in recent decades. When the demand for cheap wine fell in the 1970s, some maverick producers started a movement towards distinctive, high-quality wines, mainly white, with some from international varieties such as Chardonnay.

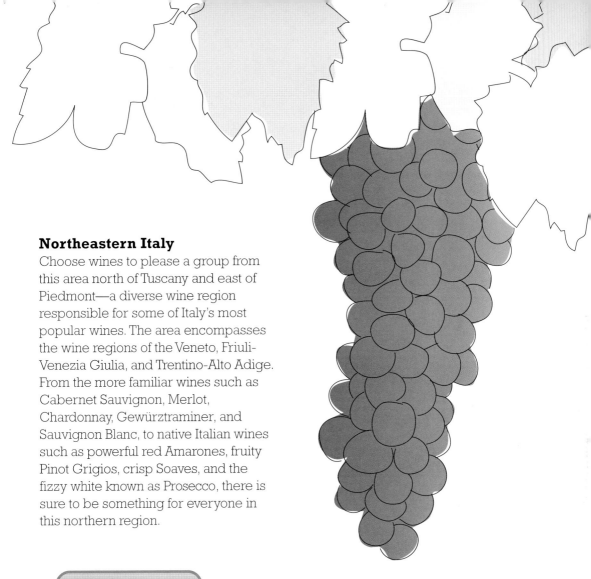

## Northeastern Italy

Choose wines to please a group from this area north of Tuscany and east of Piedmont—a diverse wine region responsible for some of Italy's most popular wines. The area encompasses the wine regions of the Veneto, Friuli-Venezia Giulia, and Trentino-Alto Adige. From the more familiar wines such as Cabernet Sauvignon, Merlot, Chardonnay, Gewürztraminer, and Sauvignon Blanc, to native Italian wines such as powerful red Amarones, fruity Pinot Grigios, crisp Soaves, and the fizzy white known as Prosecco, there is sure to be something for everyone in this northern region.

### wine buff

One of the only places outside of Italy that native Italian wine grapes are grown is half a world away in California. Around the turn of the last century, Italians fled poverty in their native country and found their way to northern California, where other Italians were settling because the terrain and climate reminded them of home. They labored on the railroads, in dairy farms or rock quarries to acquire the money needed to buy vineyards or wineries. Many of them succeeded and built wineries in the Napa Valley, Sonoma, and other parts of the state. In the 1990s, many of those wineries circled back to their Italian heritage by planting, producing, and promoting "Cal-Ital" wines made from Italian grape varieties, such as Sangiovese, Pinot Grigio, Arneis, and Nebbiolo.

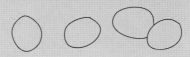

### Think Spain

Among European wine cultures, the first to come to mind may be France and Italy, but Spain is a close third. Although it is the third largest producer of wine in the world, Spain has more grapevines than any other country and its roots as a wine culture extend through thousands of years. Wine is a staple at meals, and Spanish art and religion is infused with images of the grape. There are seven major wine regions scattered throughout Spain. Tempranillo, a robust red grape, is the best-known outside of the country. Wineries are called *bodegas*, and many are open to the public for tours and free wine-tasting.

### Rioja: the king of Spain

To experience royalty, try Rioja wines. They are made mostly from a blend of the intensely flavored Tempranillo grape (usually sixty to seventy percent), Garnacha (Grenache—fifteen to twenty percent), and the rest made up of Graciano and Mazuelo. This fairly small area in the northern part of the country is the king of Spain's winegrowing regions—and one of the world's great wine producing areas. Located in north-central Spain, Rioja is a pleasant, convenient, and delicious diversion from Spain's crowded tourist meccas. The natives here take a great interest in food, wine and conviviality often until the wee hours—in true Spanish style.

### Priorato

For the cutting edge in Spanish wines, try wines from this up-and-coming Spanish wine area. Priorato is a small wine-producing area about 90 minutes' drive west of Barcelona. Thanks to some remarkable wines made by a small group of winemakers, who dubbed themselves "crazy romantics" to be making wine in the rugged, steep terrain of this area, Priorato has garnered notice for its new-style red wines, which are rich and full-bodied, with good fruit and complexity.

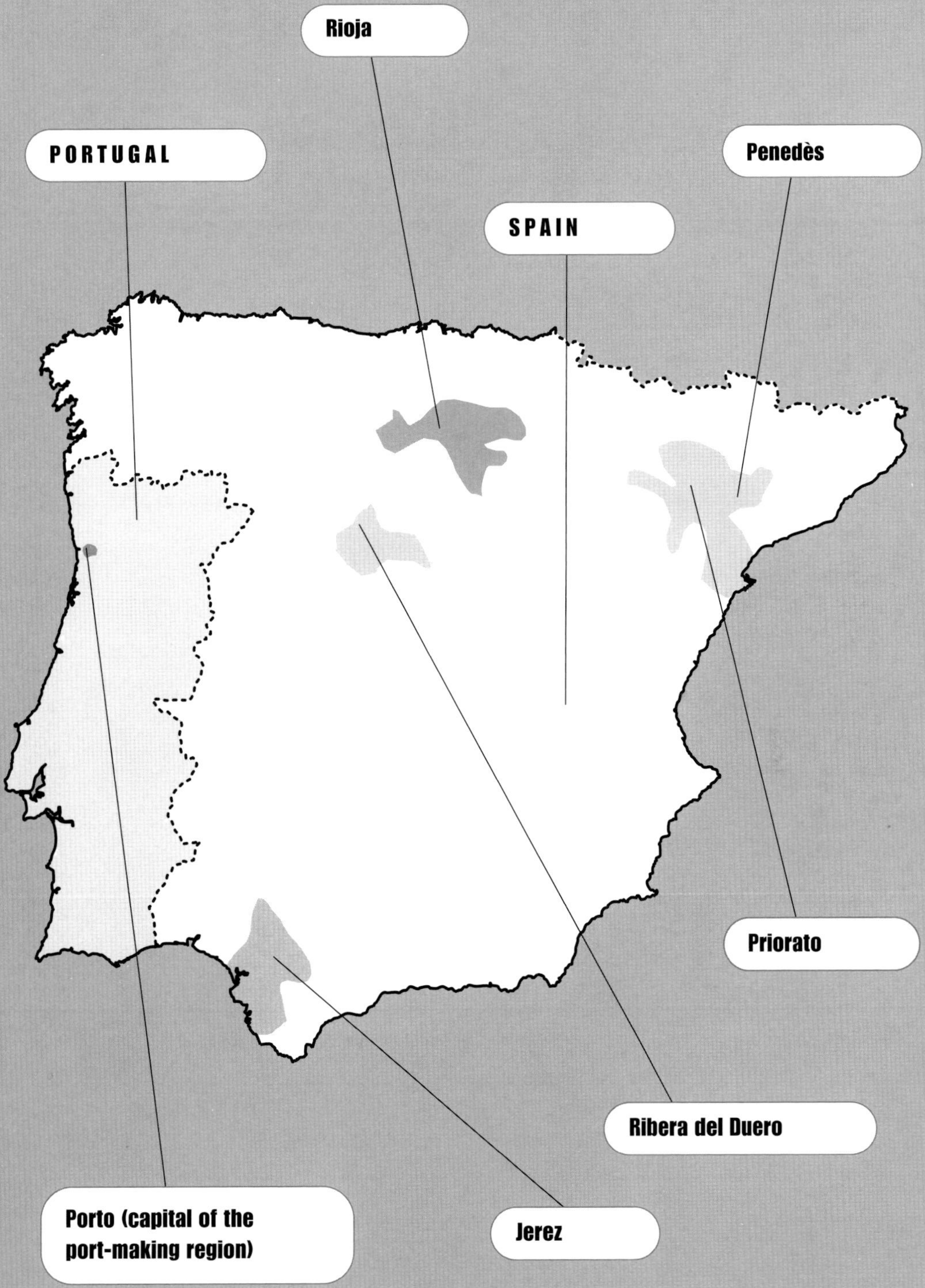

Rioja

PORTUGAL

Penedès

SPAIN

Priorato

Ribera del Duero

Porto (capital of the
port-making region)

Jerez

## Penedès, the *cava* capital

If you like your bubbly, especially at reasonable prices, try Spanish cava from this, the world-famous center of the cava industry. The Penedès region, less than an hour's drive from the dynamic, daring city of Barcelona in Catalonia, has been making sparkling white made from three grapes native to the region for hundreds of years. It is a Catalonian tradition and is especially popular in European countries. Some impressive still wines come from the Penedès area, too.

## Jerez, home of sherry

For something a little different from reds and sparkling, try Fino sherry from the place it originated. Sherry is the aperitif in Spain, and is a great partner for tapas, the delectable Spanish appetizers that can make up a whole meal. Sherry was invented in Jerez, in southwest Spain, and is imitated all over the world, but true sherry comes only from Jerez, where a certain kind of yeast, known as flor, gives the drink its unique flavor.

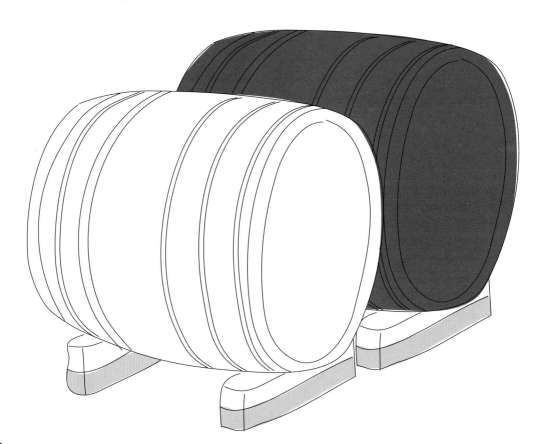

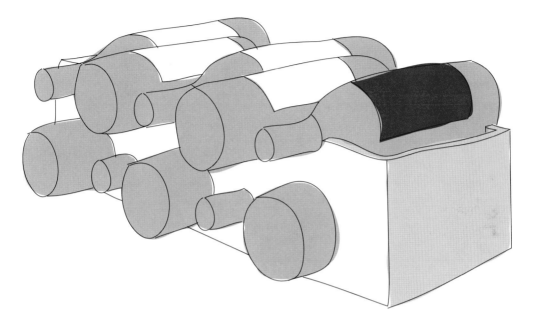

## Big reds from Ribera del Duero

If you like concentrated, fruity red wines, you will really like the wines from this wine region in north-central Spain west of Rioja. Ribera del Duero is home to one of the country's most prestigious wineries and is a great place to visit any time of year because of its outstanding natural beauty. Most of the red wines are made from Spain's mighty Tempranillo grape (known here as Tinto del País), but bodegas also blend Tempranillo with Cabernet Sauvignon, Malbec, Merlot, and Garnacha, to achieve more of a fashionable international style.

## Portugal

Look to Portugal, located southwest of Spain, for its eponymous product, port, and some respectable dry table wines—quite light, low in alcohol and perfect for midday drinking over a long lunch. Port is a fortified wine with smooth, aromatic flavors. Most ports, dark and rich, should not be drunk for ten to twenty years after bottling, but few loyal port fans probably wait that long. (White port, a treat rarely found outside the country, makes a refreshing, early-drinking aperitif when served over ice.) A bottle of port isn't cheap, but this is a slow-sipping, after-dinner wine, one that lasts for a long time and doesn't go bad after opening—brandy added to the wine stabilizes it for a long life. Madeira, named after the Portuguese island it comes from, is another fortified wine.

## Germany: a great wine country

Remember this next time you're staring at a confusing German wine label with a long, unpronounceable name: Germany makes some of the best wines in the world, especially whites. Don't be scared off! The complicated ranking system of German wines, along with those indecipherable names, have left many consumers scratching their heads and moving on to a Pinot Gris from France or a Pinot Grigio from Italy. Its greatest wine areas include the Mosel River Valley, the Rheingau, Rheinhessen, and the Pfalz, and its greatest grape is the Riesling.

## German rankings

*Tafelwein* (table wine) is the lowest quality level of wine in Germany. *Qualitätswein bestimmte Anbaugebiete* (thankfully shortened as QbA) is a step higher and classifies mid-level German wines, while *Qualitätswein mit Prädikat* (shortened as QmP) is the next and highest quality level of German wine.

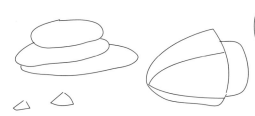

## Music to a wine-lover's ears

Austria, famous for its music scene, is often overlooked when it comes to wine, but do not commit the same error! Top wine producing areas in this landlocked country south of Germany include the Wachau, Kremstal, and Kamptal. Its fresh and fruity white wines, such as Grüner Veltliner and Riesling, are the standouts, but it also makes respectable red wines such as Blaufränkisch and Zweigelt with deep berry flavors. Austria is also renowned for its dessert wines. The top whites and dessert wines are the most expensive, but there are good value whites and reds.

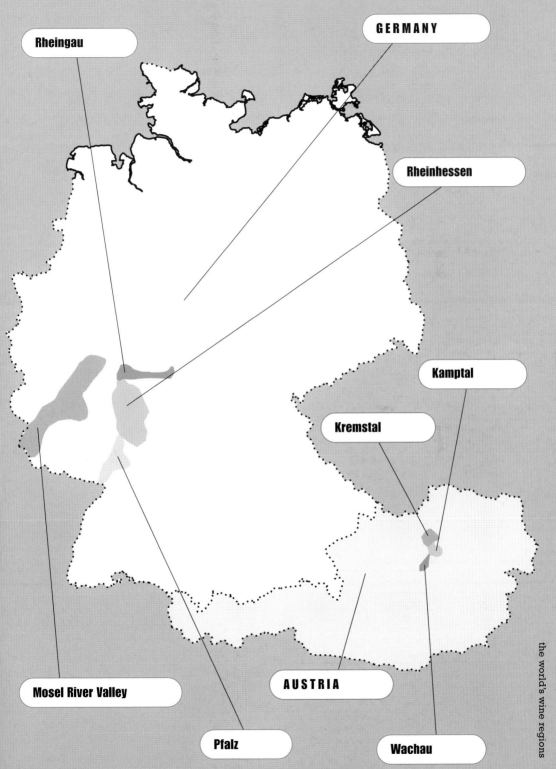

Rheingau

**GERMANY**

Rheinhessen

Kamptal

Kremstal

Mosel River Valley

**AUSTRIA**

Pfalz

Wachau

### A winery in (almost) every state

Although every state in the fifty that make up the United States has at least one winery (except for North Dakota), the wine regions that dominate the American wine industry are California, Washington, Oregon, and New York. California produces ninety percent of all U.S. wine. If it were a nation, it would be the fourth leading wine-producing country in the world, behind France, Italy, and Spain.

### The straight and narrow in Napa

Go to Napa wines to see what has made this relatively small, narrow valley the United States' best-known wine region, even though it produces only a minute portion of the state's wine output. If a wine region had a personality, Napa would be driven and straight-laced: the kid in the class who always strove to be the best. American wine pioneer Robert Mondavi established his winery here in the 1960s and tirelessly promoted Napa Valley and American wines around the world. The climate, soils, and grape farming and winemaking talent in the Napa Valley contribute to making Napa Valley wines world-class. Cabernet Sauvignon is the main attraction and the highest-priced, but Chardonnay, Sauvignon Blanc, Zinfandel, and Merlot are also widely planted and produced.

MOUNTAIN VIEW

*Napa Valley*
CHARDONNAY
1994

PRODUCED AND BOTTLED BY MOUNTAIN VIEW WINERY
ST HELENA, CA·ALC. 13.4% BY VOL·CONTAINS SULFITES

GOVERNMENT WARNING: ACCORDING TO THE SURGEON GENERAL, WOMEN SHOULD NOT DRINK ALCOHOLIC BEVERAGES DURING PREGNANCY BECAUSE OF THE RISK OF BIRTH DEFECTS. 2. CONSUMPTION OF ALCOHOLIC BEVERAGES IMPAIRS YOUR ABILITY TO DRIVE A CAR, OR OPERATE MACHINERY, AND MAY CAUSE HEALTH PROBLEMS.

### Paying top-dollar for top-drawer

If you have a taste for Napa Valley Cabernet Sauvignons, shop smart. They are generally high-priced—many times the average price for a bottle of wine from the rest of the state. If you are looking for reasonably priced Cabernets from the region, wines that say "Single Vineyard" or "Estate Bottled" on their labels will be the highest-priced. Instead, look for wines that say "Napa Valley" or "Napa County." Also, keep in mind that older, more established wineries often sell their wines at lower prices than small or new boutique wineries.

wine genius

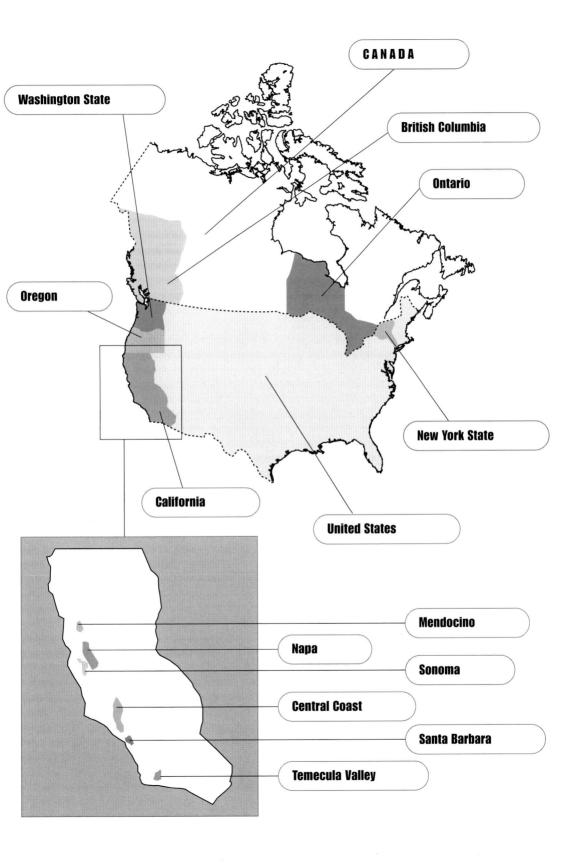

## Laid-back Sonoma

If Napa is like attending a black-tie dinner, Sonoma, its friendly next-door neighbor, is more of a frat party. As long ago as 1872, this was the number-one wine producer in the United States, surpassing Los Angeles, the California industry's birthplace. Today, Sonoma has four major grape-producing valleys and is much bigger and more diverse than Napa. It has always lagged behind Napa in promoting its wines, but they are generally on a par with Napa wines in quality, while most sport lower price tags. Sonoma's Pinot Noir from the cool Russian River Valley and Zinfandel from warmer regions are among its better wines. If Sonoma were a person, he would be the one in the Aloha shirt and sandals, with a knack for mixing up some divine concoctions.

## Quirky Mendocino

When you're in for a bit of a bohemian adventure, try wines from colorful Mendocino, a beautiful coastal area north of Sonoma and Napa, long overshadowed by its more famous winemaking neighbors. Locals, who might answer to "Sunshine" or "Rainbow," even invented their own language to keep outsiders at bay, and there are more than a few growers of crops that aren't quite legal, especially in the more isolated inland areas. But the Anderson Valley, close to the cooling effects of the Pacific Ocean and therefore ideal for sparkling wine, Chardonnay, and Pinot Noir, puts out wines that compete with the best anywhere. Some wineries also make excellent Zinfandel, Sauvignon Blanc, and Gewürztraminer. Because of its dramatic rocky coastline and laid-back atmosphere, the region is a really good choice for a visit.

## California's Central Coast

Shop California Central Coast wines for good value. The Central Coast of California used to be known as the vast nothingness between San Francisco and Los Angeles. Now, the Monterey and San Luis Obispo areas are reputable wine-producers, with the added bonus of lower prices than most of Napa and Sonoma's wine. The coastal location means Chardonnay and Pinot Noir, two grape types that benefit from cool weather and coastal mists, thrive here. In the Paso Robles area, Sauvignon Blanc, Syrah, and Cabernet Sauvignon also do well. Look for wines from the Edna Valley.

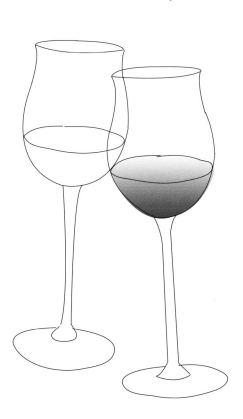

## Santa Barbara

You'll want to try the area's Chardonnay and Pinot Noir since this is a coastal area just north of Los Angeles that benefits from cooler weather, and is kind to those two cool-climate grapes. Other wines that are Santa Barbara success stories are Rhône varieties, such as Grenache, Syrah, and Viognier. Missionaries first brought grapevines to bucolic Santa Barbara county in southern California in the 1770s. But for the past 100 years it has been known more for Gucci than Grenache because of its reputation as a playground for the Hollywood rich. Today, the area encompasses two dynamic wine-growing regions—the dominant Santa Maria Valley and its smaller colleague, the Santa Ynez Valley—and over seventy wineries.

## Temecula Valley

Try the respectable to very good wines made here with lower price tags than many other area of California. The Temecula Valley is small wine-country region of vineyards, ranches, and foothills one hour from both Los Angeles and San Diego in southern California. The region was hard-hit in the late 1990s by a vineyard pest that destroyed about a third of its vineyards. Although California's first grapes were planted here by Spanish missionaries some 200 years ago, most of the wineries are fairly new. Wines to look out for include Cabernet Sauvignon plus interesting whites such as Viognier and Pinot Gris.

## Oregon

Pinot Noir is the star wine of this state. When Bob Dylan wrote "A hard rain is gonna fall!" he was probably in Oregon wine country. Unfortunately, when the clouds let loose during the fall harvest, the rainfall can jeopardize the entire area's wine output—thus the quality of Oregon wines varies from year to year more so than its neighbor to the north, Washington, and its southern neighbor, California. Yet when the harvest is good, Oregon wines can be excellent. Besides a multitude of delicious Pinot Noirs, Cabernet Sauvignon and Merlot are also worth trying. For white-wine-lovers, taste Pinot Gris, rapidly becoming an Oregon specialty.

## Washington State

Cabernet Sauvignon, Cabernet blends, Merlot, Chardonnay, and a variety of dessert wines made from Riesling, Gewürztraminer, and Sémillon are the standouts in this Pacific northwest state. One of the nation's youngest winemaking states, Washington is considered by many to rank second only to California. Areas producing quality wines include Walla Walla, the Yakima Valley, and the Puget Sound.

## Wine? In New York?

It's only a cottage industry, but vintners from New York's Long Island, which juts out into the Atlantic ocean, are making some of the state's best wines—wines that are commanding the attention and the allegiance of some of New York City's most high-toned restaurants. The Long Island wine industry boasts a maritime climate and mild winters. A few dozen vintners have planted grapevines in former potato fields, with very good results. Chardonnay, Merlot, rosé, and sparkling wines are all worth trying. A considerably older wine industry dating to the early 1800s is located upstate in the Finger Lakes region, which turns out some delicate dry white wines such as Riesling, plus dessert and ice wines. In the 1990s, the Finger Lakes area experienced a boom in boutique wineries.

## British Columbia

Canada's wine regions have it all: open landscapes, plentiful sunshine for ripening grapes to their optimum, high-quality wines, and great value due to favorable exchange rates. Some of the leading high-quality wines produced in the Okanagan Valley, one of Canada's two major wine regions, include aromatic and delicate white wines such as Riesling and Pinot Blanc. In British Columbia, many European immigrants to the south. Okanagan have developed vineyards and wineries in a climate similar to that of the north of France. Within a 150-mile range, marked with blue-and-white ''Wine Route'' highway signs, there are about forty wineries, with free tours and wine tastings. There are wine biking tours and major wine festivals.

## Ontario

If you are an ice-wine devotee, look to Ontario, the other high-quality wine area that has emerged in Canada. Even some French vintners are buying wineries and producing wine here. Notable wines include Cabernet Sauvignon and Merlot, along with whites such as Gewürztraminer, Chardonnay, Riesling, and Pinot Blanc. But the star product of this area may well be ice wine, made principally in the Ontario region due to its consistently cold climate. This dessert wine is deep and rich in both aroma and flavor. Canada exports about fifteen percent of its wine to foreign markets, including the United Kingdom, Japan, China, and the United States, so you do not have to visit to enjoy them.

## The Southern Hemisphere

### Awesome Australia

Look to Australian wines for big statements. The country's trademark wines are its generally inky Shiraz (Aussie talk for the French Syrah) and oily Chardonnay; the Australian way is to make them powerful and highly flavored. Australian wines have assaulted the world marketplace with high-quality products at reasonable prices. Its group of winemakers—an adventurous, experimental lot—have been found soaking up the local wine culture everywhere from France to Napa and taking what they learn back to their home industry. This huge, dynamic country has a handful of expansive wine regions and produces an amount of wine that is growing at phenomenal rates due in no small part to their good value. An up-and-coming wine to look out for from Australia is another French grape variety: Grenache.

### Notable niches

The major wine-producing regions of Australia to look out for include Victoria, South Australia, where the notable Barossa Valley and Coonawarra are located, Western Australia, home to the Margaret River district, and New South Wales, location of the Hunter Valley. The high-altitude vineyard area of Orange, the epicenter of the country's nineteenth-century gold rush, is today an emerging wine area on a higher level: literally 2,000 to 3,000 feet.

### New Zealand: Kiwi wines

This country's major wine stars are Sauvignon Blanc and Pinot Noir. European settlers planted the first vines here in the early 1800s, but it was only in the late twentieth century that New Zealand started producing distinctive, high-quality wines that won international notice and admiration. The country is the world's most southerly (and also among the coolest wine regions,)—but that only makes it all the more appealing to New Zealand's adventurous vintners. Known for Sauvignon Blanc, New Zealand is appreciated for both its high quality and good value. In the Central Otago region, Pinot Noirs are fetching high prices and high praise. There are three main growing regions in new Zealand—Marlborough, Hawke's Bay, and Gisborne—and you'll find more than 300 wineries, many of them trendy, well regarded boutiques.

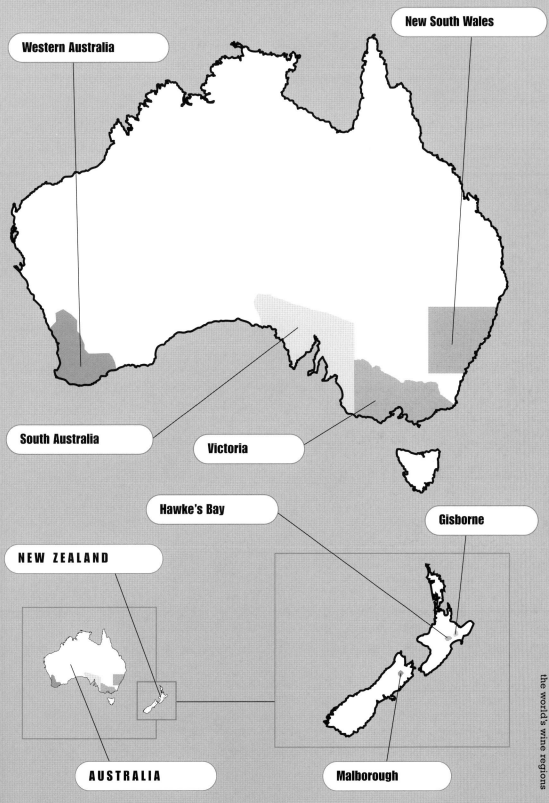

Western Australia

New South Wales

South Australia

Victoria

Hawke's Bay

Gisborne

NEW ZEALAND

AUSTRALIA

Malborough

## Chile

Go Chilean for good value and wines that stand up to many made in the more established wine regions of the world. The wine industry in Chile dates back to the sixteenth century, but it wasn't until the 1990s that Chilean wineries began to bring their winemaking up to world-class standards. The country now produces and sells wines around the world that range from luxury-class to extremely affordable, yet almost all are high-quality. Wine-producing regions to look for include Maipo, Aconcagua, Colchagua, and Casablanca. Some of the best grapes grown in Chile include Cabernet Franc, Syrah, Malbec, Merlot, and Carmenère, a hearty red wine. Bordeaux-style blends made from Cabernet Sauvignon, Merlot, and Cabernet Franc are also common. Wineries do not have a long history of receiving guests, but most large ones now conduct tours and wine tasting for visitors.

## Getting high in Argentina

Try Argentine Malbec. It is Argentina's strong suit, much of it grown in the high-altitude vineyards of Mendoza, a high desert region that is the country's best wine-producing area. Malbec, a wine grape used to blend with others in Bordeaux, now stands largely on its own, though it is sometimes blended with Cabernet Sauvignon. Other wines worth trying include Syrah, Bonarda (similar to the Italian Barbera), Chardonnay, and Torrontes, a spicy Muscat-like grape native to Argentina and similar to Gewürztraminer. As with Chilean wines, you will also enjoy the lower price tags on many of these Argentine wines.

## South Africa

Always look for Stellenbosch on any bottle of South African wine. This is the premier winemaking region in South Africa located outside coastal Cape Town at the very tip of the African continent. It is fast gaining a reputation as a beautiful wine-country region to visit and a quality producer of elegant wines. Stellenbosch makes excellent wines from the Sauvignon Blanc grape in a crisp, lean style. Other wines produced in this region include Chardonnay, Merlot, Cabernet Sauvignon, and a local red wine, Pinotage (a red grape that is a cross of Pinot Noir and Cinsault). Although not accepted in wine circles outside of South Africa in the past, wines made from Pinotage at many Stellenbosch wineries are fast gaining international appeal.

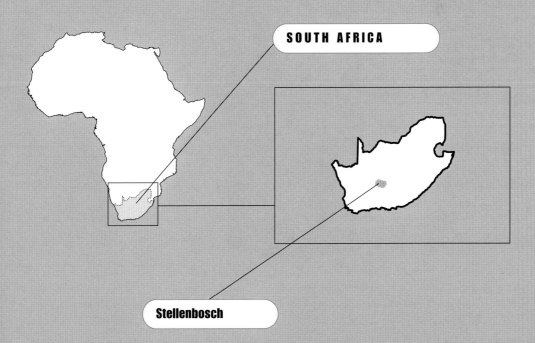

CHILE

ARGENTINA

Maipo, Aconcagua, Colchagua, Casablanca

Mendoza

SOUTH AFRICA

Stellenbosch

# index

index

**255**

# Acknowledgements

Drink recipes kindly supplied by:

Barry Wiss, of Trinchero Family Estates, St. Helena, California.

Marimar Torres, Marimar Torres Estate, Sebastopol, California.

Domaine Chandon, Yountville, California.

Beringer Vineyards, St. Helena, California.